# little brand book

# little brand book

Find Your Inner InfluenceHer
to Work It, Own It, Bring It

Kalika Yap

HARPER
DESIGN

An Imprint of HarperCollinsPublishers

My family is the foundation from which I can dream.
It's their endless support that keeps me grounded and
flying at the same time.

Thank you.

This book is dedicated to Ederlina Nacion for teaching
me love, grit, and light.

# Contents

# the 12 major archetypes

# the irl influencesters

# hello, boss!

There's nothing little about this book. It's packed full of big branding tips to help you understand and elevate your brand. It will give you the foundation to grow your business, career, and life.

Whether you're the founder of a start-up or a global CEO who wants to stay relevant—this book will help you.

This book was inspired by you: my fellow female founders who have faced inequality, limited opportunity, and obstacles that our male counterparts have never seen. I've been there with you. I've muddled through the trenches of business and have come out on the other side with a passion to share this branding and business know-how.

Orange & Bergamot was born out of this desire to help women business owners with their branding and interactive design needs. I've taken my twenty years of experience owning a design agency and distilled the branding process into a simple quiz that will tell you about you and your business core essence.

And that is Lesson #1: Always stay true to your "why." My why is:

> **1 million dreams**
> **1 million female founders changing the world**
> **1 million jobs created**

*Little Brand Book* is my first contribution (of many to come) to the wave of women empowerment.

With a simple framework to better understand the power of you and how you can shine, you will be able to work it, own it, bring it in every experience you create.

Let's do this!

Kalika

"Figuring out who you are is the whole point of the human experience."

Anna Quindlen

# how to use this book

For those of you on the go, go, go, here's a quick guide to get you started. Dive right in and have some fun!

*first...*      Get centered. Take a deep breath and align with your authentic self. Read the **Brand Boss Code** to help you understand how the twelve major archetypes apply to your company, life, career, and even relationships.

*then...*      Time to take the **Brand Quiz**. This test will help you find out what your major and minor archetypes are. The combination of the two make up one of 144 archetypes.

*finally...*      Flip through the pages and discover your **Brand Boss Archetype** and get a few tips on how to work it, own it, bring it!

*for fun...*      Share the brand test! Have some fun and check out the other archetypes to get more tips and understand your fellow **Brand Bosses**! Make a game of it with your friends and colleagues and have them take the test, too!

*hollah!*

*Look out for **Bonus Material** worksheets and tips that can be found on our website orangeandbergamot.com/bonus*

maven

heroine

idealist

bff

gem

explorer

leader

brilliant

original

rebel

world changer

charismatic

# the brand boss code

---

Let's play a game. Walk up to a mirror and what do you see? Besides thinking, "Damn, I look good!" What else do you see? Do you see the real you? Your authentic self?

And if so, do you know how to work it to help you be your best and thrive in business, life, and relationships?

Well, lucky for you, you have this book. I know that in today's crazy, insane world, we need to know why it matters. Only then can you align with the right audience, build trust, and, ultimately, brand devotion (aka your peeps, your squad, your tribe!).

What does it mean to be authentic? We need to dive deeper to discover who we are and what we do best.

**The Brand Boss Code** is based on twelve major archetypes that every brand and person fits within. For example, when the line for the bathroom is ginormous and you say, "Screw that. I'm going to the men's room! It may be nasty, but I'm breaking ranks," you're pulling a Rebel move. And it may be a part of your core archetype—the Rebel!

Your **Brand Boss Archetype** is a combination of your major and minor archetypes. Who really fits into one mold anyway? Doing the math, we end up with a total of 144 Brand Boss Archetypes.

Curious?

Read on.

# the 12 major archetypes

First, let's get to know the major archetypes. They're broken into four sub-groups that will help assess the core of your personality: the sages, seekers, sparks, and soul sisters.

## sages
information-oriented

 **maven**
Our teachers. They are virtuosos in their field. They are fulfilled by sharing knowledge with others.

 **brilliant**
Our intellectuals. We find them constantly observing and analyzing the world around them. Show them the data and facts and spare them the emotional sideshow.

 **original**
Our creatives. They see the world through their playful imagination. Whether it's to improve others' ideas or dream up something never seen before, they are eager to share their gift.

## seekers
idea-oriented

 **idealist**
Our eternal optimists. Their positivity is infectious. They are visionaries who see all the good in the world and what could be.

 **world changer**
Our innovators. They're our change agents for good. They push beyond what is and create electrifying change in the world.

 **explorer**
Our journeywomen. Their enthusiasm and curiosity guide them to forge new paths.

## sparks
action-oriented

 **heroine**
Our rock stars. They're head turners in a crowded room. The kind who others look to and admire.

 **leader**
Our go-getters. Always chasing perfection and seeking to do their best, they feel at peace when they're checking off items on their goals list. The get-it-done types.

 **rebel**
Our challengers. They question everything. They go against the grain.

## soul sisters
people-oriented

 **bff**
Our trusted allies. These are our wing-women. They have our back, no questions asked.

 **gem**
Our nurturers. They are our security blankets, taking care of everyone with love and support.

 **charismatic**
Our fun-lovers. Their humor and positivity are infectious to be around.

# the brand boss quiz

STEP 1. **TAKE THE TEST. IT'S EASY**
Circle all attributes that describe your brand personality. The goal is to find out which groupings you have the most attributes in. Take the full test on our website orangeandbergamot.com/brand-quiz.

## 1 maven

Patient

Communicative

Intelligent

Empowering

Wise

Intuitive

## 4 idealist

Innocent

Optimistic

Hopeful

Joyful

Dreamy

Free-spirited

## 2 brilliant

Factual

Inquisitive

Analytical

Insightful

Intellectual

Rational

## 5 world changer

Resourceful

Advocative

Determined

Justice-oriented

Activist

Initiative-taker

## 3 original

Creative

Inspired

Artistic

Pondering

Sophisticated

Tasteful

## 6 explorer

Adventurous

Fearless

Curious

On the move

Globetrotting

Experience-seeking

*write your results here ⟶

STEP 2. **THE MOMENT OF TRUTH**
The grouping in which you have the MOST attributes is your major archetype. The second-most is your minor archetype. Now on to the next page to determine your Brand Boss Archetype.

## 7 heroine
- Resilient
- Passionate
- Courageous
- Competitive
- Unstoppable
- Inspirational

## 10 bff
- Trustworthy
- Reliable
- Loving
- Loyal
- Consistent
- Humble

## 8 leader
- Powerful
- Ambitious
- Productive
- Driven
- Hardworking
- Self-motivated

## 11 gem
- Authentic
- Resourceful
- Warm
- Caring
- Kind
- Empathetic

## 9 rebel
- Challenger
- Independent
- Free thinking
- Unapologetic
- Brave
- Avant-garde

## 12 charismatic
- Energizing
- Fascinating
- Irresistible
- Entertaining
- Funny
- Captivating

your major archetype:

_____

your minor archetype:

_____

| your major | X | your minor | = | your archetype | pg. |
|---|---|---|---|---|---|
| **1** maven | | MAVEN | | Sage | 24 |
| | | WORLD CHANGER | | Educator | 25 |
| | | IDEALIST | | Hopeful | 26 |
| | | EXPLORER | | Pilot | 27 |
| | | HEROINE | | Laurel | 28 |
| | | LEADER | | Master | 29 |
| | | BRILLIANT | | Professor | 30 |
| | | REBEL | | Critic | 31 |
| | | BFF | | Coach | 32 |
| | | GEM | | Inspiration | 33 |
| | | ORIGINAL | | Luminary | 34 |
| | | CHARISMATIC | | Correspondent | 35 |

| your major | X | your minor | = | your archetype | pg. |
|---|---|---|---|---|---|
| **2** brilliant | | MAVEN | | Philosopher | 40 |
| | | WORLD CHANGER | | Egalitarian | 41 |
| | | IDEALIST | | Prodigy | 42 |
| | | EXPLORER | | Alchemist | 43 |
| | | HEROINE | | Remarkable | 44 |
| | | LEADER | | Innovator | 45 |
| | | BRILLIANT | | Intellectual | 46 |
| | | REBEL | | Whiz | 47 |
| | | BFF | | Realist | 48 |
| | | GEM | | Allocator | 49 |
| | | ORIGINAL | | Poet | 50 |
| | | CHARISMATIC | | Geek | 51 |

| your major | X | your minor | = | your archetype | pg. |
|---|---|---|---|---|---|
| **3** original | | MAVEN | | Curator | 56 |
| | | WORLD CHANGER | | Creator | 57 |
| | | IDEALIST | | Ponderer | 58 |
| | | EXPLORER | | Novelist | 59 |
| | | HEROINE | | Celestial | 60 |
| | | LEADER | | Composer | 61 |
| | | BRILLIANT | | Architect | 62 |
| | | REBEL | | Firecracker | 63 |
| | | BFF | | Classicist | 64 |
| | | GEM | | Affectionate | 65 |
| | | ORIGINAL | | Virtuoso | 66 |
| | | CHARISMATIC | | Playful | 67 |

| your major | X | your minor | = | your archetype | pg. |
|---|---|---|---|---|---|
| **10** bff | | MAVEN | | Principal | 168 |
| | | WORLD CHANGER | | Changemaker | 169 |
| | | IDEALIST | | Anchor | 170 |
| | | EXPLORER | | Curious | 171 |
| | | HEROINE | | Magnificent | 172 |
| | | LEADER | | Dependable | 173 |
| | | BRILLIANT | | Level Head | 174 |
| | | REBEL | | Vanguard | 175 |
| | | BFF | | Confidante | 176 |
| | | GEM | | Mainstay | 177 |
| | | ORIGINAL | | Artisan | 178 |
| | | CHARISMATIC | | Popular | 179 |

| your major | X | your minor | = | your archetype | pg. |
|---|---|---|---|---|---|
| **11** gem | | MAVEN | | Counselor | 184 |
| | | WORLD CHANGER | | Ally | 185 |
| | | IDEALIST | | Companion | 186 |
| | | EXPLORER | | Cultivator | 187 |
| | | HEROINE | | Altruist | 188 |
| | | LEADER | | First Lady | 189 |
| | | BRILLIANT | | Dean | 190 |
| | | REBEL | | Authentic | 191 |
| | | BFF | | Royal Citizen | 192 |
| | | GEM | | Humanitarian | 193 |
| | | ORIGINAL | | Stylist | 194 |
| | | CHARISMATIC | | Angel | 195 |

| your major | X | your minor | = | your archetype | pg. |
|---|---|---|---|---|---|
| **12** charismatic | | MAVEN | | Friendly Savant | 200 |
| | | WORLD CHANGER | | Good Citizen | 201 |
| | | IDEALIST | | Rosy | 202 |
| | | EXPLORER | | Open Heart | 203 |
| | | HEROINE | | Catalyst | 204 |
| | | LEADER | | Influencer | 205 |
| | | BRILLIANT | | Wit | 206 |
| | | REBEL | | Funny Girl | 207 |
| | | BFF | | Darling | 208 |
| | | GEM | | Spark | 209 |
| | | ORIGINAL | | Dynamo | 210 |
| | | CHARISMATIC | | Entertainer | 211 |

"As you become more clear about who you really are, you'll be better able to decide what's best for you— the first time around."

Oprah

MAJOR ARCHETYPE

# maven

1

You're a seeker of truth and understanding. You're constantly learning, and people flock to you for advice and counsel. You're a fountainhead of knowledge and respected in your area of expertise.

Because of your treasure trove of knowledge, you see patterns and are highly discerning and intuitive.

Get to know the sound of your own inner voice. Be magnificent. Be creative. Be bold.

**Key Attributes:**

Empowering
Truth-Seeking
Curious
Diligent
Wise

Emotionally Intelligent
Aware
Enthusiastic
Respected

# Brand mastery

**maven**
sage

**world changer**
educator

**idealist**
hopeful

**explorer**
pilot

**heroine**
laurel

**leader**
master

**brilliant**
professor

**rebel**
critic

**bff**
coach

**gem**
inspiration

**original**
luminary

**charismatic**
correspondent

*Your brand mastery*

# sage

⊗ maven      x     ⊗ maven

A guide through and through. Your passion is to share what you know with others. As soon as you learn something new, you can't wait to show a friend. You're respected and a source of knowledge for everyone around you. A TED Talk is in your future.

*Work it...*

**You are powerful because you are:**

- Wise
- Astute
- Awe-inspiring
- A confident presenter
- A lifelong learner

*Own it...*

**Get inspired by these kindred brands:**

NPR, TED Talks

*Bring it...*

**Amplify your strengths:**

Utilize social media to reach a wider audience and share your tips and knowledge.

*Your brand mastery*

# educator

 maven       x       🌐 world changer

You believe the best way to make a positive impact on the future is to instruct those who are a part of it. As a result, you're an active participant in educating the next generation. You use practical yet innovative teaching methods to maximize the results of your instruction.

*Work it...*

**You are powerful because you are:**

- Optimistic
- Innovative
- Faithful
- Learned
- Good at explaining concepts in a digestible way

*Own it...*

**Get inspired by these kindred brands:**

Maria Montessori, Bill & Melinda Gates Foundation

*Bring it...*

**Amplify your strengths:**

Using the latest technology can help propel your knowledge to a wider audience. Also, find techniques to keep your audience fully engaged. Make an impact today and every day.

# hopeful

 maven X ♡ idealist

You're committed to educating others because of the positive way in which you view the future. You've realized that the more people you enlighten, the more your energy will be spread throughout the world.

*Work it...* **You are powerful because you are:**

- Optimistic
- A part of something bigger than yourself
- Willing to share knowledge with the world
- Someone who knows that people have different learning styles
- Empathetic and gentle

*Own it...* **Get inspired by these kindred brands:**

Jackie O, Emily Dickinson

*Bring it...* **Amplify your strengths:**

Your messages should always be positive and encouraging, which will persuade your followers to pay attention.

*Your brand mastery*

# pilot

maven    X    explorer

Charting a course to assist others in their journey for knowledge is a key driver for you. You're inspired by the pursuit and exploration of wisdom. You experience life and share what you know.

*Work it...*

### You are powerful because you are:

- Someone who gets your knowledge firsthand and not exclusively through books
- One who explores learning through sensory experiences
- Excited about the unfolding of the future
- Boldly inquisitive

*Own it...*

### Get inspired by these kindred brands:

Amelia Earhart, Travel Channel

*Bring it...*

### Amplify your strengths:

Enhance your knowledge by using all of your five senses. Dive into neurolinguistic programming and see if you're a kinesthetic, visual, or auditory learner.

*Your brand mastery*

# laurel

maven    X    heroine

You're an authentic role model for others. People are naturally attracted to you for your strength and confidence. You're a fantastic leader, and your can-do attitude and accomplishments are attributes others would like to emulate.

## Work it...

**You are powerful because you are:**

- Uplifting
- Fearless
- Passionate
- Gifted
- A leader by example

## Own it...

**Get inspired by these kindred brands:**

Maya Angelou, Toni Morrison

## Bring it...

**Amplify your strengths:**

Carefully figure out what message you would like to share with others. Live that and be vocal about it. You inspire others with your boldness and willingness to speak out about causes greater than yourself.

*Your brand mastery*

# master

⊛ maven    X    ▷ leader

Through your life experiences, studies, and observations, you have become an expert in your chosen passion. People consistently come to you for your expertise.

*Work it...*

**You are powerful because you are:**

- Eager to spread your knowledge
- Composed
- Confident
- A virtuoso in your field
- Proficient

*Own it...*

**Get inspired by these kindred brands:**

MasterClass, Lynda Weinman

*Bring it...*

**Amplify your strengths:**

Start a podcast, blog, or online class to share your wealth of knowledge with others. People are interested in learning from you.

# professor

maven    X    brilliant

Nerds rule! Your passion for teaching is equal to your desire to soak up knowledge as you go. You're studious and focused on your area of expertise. Your learning never stops as you are always trying to master the subject.

*Work it...*

**You are powerful because you are:**

- Analytical
- Tuned in
- Focused on the project at hand
- Always questioning and pursuing answers
- Passionate about teaching others what you know

*Own it...*

**Get inspired by these kindred brands:**

*The New Yorker, Psychology Today*

*Bring it...*

**Amplify your strengths:**

Your trick is to get everything in your head out to others in a clear, digestible, step-by-step format. Remember, you might know it, but you can't assume that others do, too.

# critic

 maven X ⚡ rebel

For you, honesty is the best policy. You tell it like it is and you rarely censor yourself when sharing with others. You believe everyone has the right to know the truth, and you are vigilant in communicating that.

*Work it...*

**You are powerful because you are:**

• Candid
• Versed
• Constructive
• Virtuous
• Unconventional

*Own it...*

**Get inspired by these kindred brands:**

Tarana Burke, Katharine Hepburn

*Bring it...*

**Amplify your strengths:**

Not every truthful scenario is the same. Be mindful of others' thoughts and feelings when spilling your advice and comments. Steer clear of the negative and always make sure you provide critiques wrapped in a positive tone.

## Your brand mastery
# coach

⊗ maven    X    🛡 bff

Perched high upon the mountain, you are the one people seek for answers. Your spiritual guidance is always calm and not pushy. There is truth and wisdom in you.

*Work it...*

**You are powerful because you are:**

- Intuitive
- Amicable
- Honest
- Equitable
- Trustworthy

*Own it...*

**Get inspired by these kindred brands:**

Rachel Hollis, Marie Forleo

*Bring it...*

**Amplify your strengths:**

You know how to give great advice and you're able to see patterns of behavior in others because you've lived it yourself. You organize information in a friendly and authentic way that allows people to effortlessly embrace and understand it.

*Your brand mastery*

# inspiration

 maven    X    gem

You're the one others seek based on your prowess and past successes. Others want to learn how you did what you did and follow carefully in your footsteps. You encourage others to reach for the best within themselves.

*Work it...*

**You are powerful because you are:**

- Energized to help others
- Willing to pay it forward by sharing your experiences
- Emotionally intelligent
- One who can envision someone's potential to be the best

*Own it...*

**Get inspired by these kindred brands:**

Oprah Winfrey, Diane Sawyer

*Bring it...*

**Amplify your strengths:**

Amid the chaos of life, learn to sit still so you can feel the sparks of knowledge and inspiration deep within. When you're mindful, you can capture these sparks. The end goal? Share them with others.

# luminary

 maven  X  🈯 original

You're a true artist who looks for ways to enlighten others through your creativity. People pursue you for your imagination and vision. Your unique take on the world is invaluable.

*Work it...*

**You are powerful because you are:**

- Inventive
- Quick to discern and teach new concepts
- Energetic
- Respected in your field
- Spunky

*Own it...*

**Get inspired by these kindred brands:**

Diana Vreeland, Anna Wintour

*Bring it...*

**Amplify your strengths:**

You are full of amazing ideas that others value tremendously. Be sure to share your thoughts widely through multiple mediums.

*Your brand mastery*

# correspondent

 maven  X  charismatic

You know a lot of stuff. Not only do you know it, but you're able to break knowledge up into small pieces that everyone can understand. Your personable demeanor allows others to engage with you and learn.

*Work it...*

**You are powerful because you are:**

- Enthusiastic
- Fun
- Able to simplify any material for others
- Talkative
- Eloquent

*Own it...*

**Get inspired by these kindred brands:**

Maria Shriver, Gayle King

*Bring it...*

**Amplify your strengths:**

Don't copy other people's style. Be confident in being you. Your effervescent style will automatically attract the right audience to you. Keep at it. Don't give up if you don't get results right away.

IRL_influenceHer

# Lauren
# Messiah

Founder, School of Style
@laurenmessiah

**Why we think Lauren is the perfect Maven:**
If you hope to be the stylist to the stars, you need to bring your creative A game to the office every day. Lauren brings her It-girl fashion sense to women around the world. She is the CEO of School of Style, which teaches others how to break into the personal stylist business. She was voted by YouTube as a #WomenToWatch for her videos and courses that help women find their personal style. She is here to educate the world and share her knowledge of style to all. She is a Coach and Laurel of style.

**What branding tips would you give to a female founder?**
Get very clear on who you are serving first. All of my branding fell perfectly into place after I clearly defined my ideal client. Solid branding made it easier to communicate and connect with my clients, which ultimately resulted in more sales.

Also, you can't fake the funk, especially if you're the face of your brand. There is a lot of pressure to follow branding trends and to take on the persona of other influential people. Don't do it! People are smart; they can see right through it. Be true to yourself and your mission because people are eager to be served by someone just like you.

**What habits keep you on track?**
The more successful I become in business, the more I realize how important it is to have a regular morning routine. I wake up around 5 a.m., meditate, read or listen to something inspiring, and work out. All of those activities are non-negotiable because they set my day up for success.

Another habit I practice is to go outside of my comfort zone regularly. If I'm too comfy and cozy, that means I'm not changing and growing. A little discomfort won't kill you.

**What's the best piece of advice you would give to an entrepreneur?**
Focus, be patient, and don't give up too soon. I've worked with thousands of young women who aspire to quit their day jobs in pursuit of their passion for entrepreneurship. The biggest mistake I see them make is throwing in the towel too soon because their idea didn't get them rich right away. Your big break is coming; you have to stay the course.

"**My mother told me to be a lady. And for her, that meant be your own person, be independent.**"

Ruth Bader Ginsburg

MAJOR ARCHETYPE

# brilliant

**2**

You have an insatiable curiosity and thirst for knowledge. A whiz at *Jeopardy!* you love facts and data. You even enjoy the process of compiling information. Despite how some may view you as nerdy, your big brain is valued and admired.

**Key Attributes:**

Introspective
Observant
Insightful

Intellectual
Astute

*brand mastery*

**maven**
philosopher

**world changer**
egalitarian

**idealist**
prodigy

**explorer**
alchemist

**heroine**
remarkable

**leader**
innovator

**brilliant**
intellectual

**rebel**
whiz

**bff**
realist

**gem**
allocator

**original**
poet

**charismatic**
geek

# philosopher

 brilliant    X    maven

You are constantly observing the world around you and asking big questions. You have the ability to see the 30,000-foot view and are able to whittle that down to a single thought. You're skilled at making connections and examining them with logic and pragmatism.

*Work it...*

**You are powerful because you are:**

- Examining
- Well-informed
- Innovative
- Thirsty for knowledge
- Curious

*Own it...*

**Get inspired by these kindred brands:**

Ayn Rand, Sappho

*Bring it...*

**Amplify your strengths:**

Don't get lost in your own thoughts. Your ideas need to be shared with others in a way they understand. An openness to alternative ideas to your own will ultimately strengthen your concepts.

# egalitarian

 brilliant    X    🌐    world changer

You're an abstract thinker. You possess the creativity and perseverance to problem-solve. Like an absentminded professor, your focus is laser-like, and you're able to shut out the world around you. You work for the greater good.

*Work it...*

**You are powerful because you are:**

- Someone who believes in a higher purpose
- Riveted by the task at hand
- Perseverant
- Brilliant
- Able to take novel approaches to life's greatest mysteries

*Own it...*

**Get inspired by these kindred brands:**

Katherine Johnson, Institute for the Future

*Bring it...*

**Amplify your strengths:**

Take the time to show others your thought process in a methodical way. Always show humility and grace when demonstrating your intelligence to others.

# *Your brand mastery*
# prodigy

💡 brilliant    X    🖤 idealist

Your brain doesn't have a "power off" button, but you find that this gets you ahead. Your ability to analyze every situation with empathy is what sets you apart from the rest. You like looking on the bright side.

*Work it...*

**You are powerful because you are:**

- Inquiring
- Analytical
- Compassionate
- Prudent
- Astute

*Own it...*

**Get inspired by these kindred brands:**

Marie Curie, Amal Clooney

*Bring it...*

**Amplify your strengths:**

Learn to not overanalyze every situation. You have to find out when to get out of your head and when to trust your intuition. Find the right outlet to publish your ideas. Share your gift.

*Your brand mastery*

# alchemist

💡 brilliant    X    🧭 explorer

You are a lover of details and enjoy completing daunting tasks. You are always seeking answers and find challenges fun and exciting. You are known for seeing the unseeable and making the invisible visible.

*Work it...*    **You are powerful because you are:**

- Questioning
- Independent
- Self-guided
- Tactful
- Full of energy

*Own it...*    **Get inspired by these kindred brands:**

Chloë Sevigny, Eyewitness Travel Guides

*Bring it...*    **Amplify your strengths:**

Expand the horizons of others who may not have thought about or understood your area of expertise. Your wealth of knowledge could unlock others' curiosity. ABT. Always be teaching.

*Your brand mastery*

# remarkable

💡 brilliant   X   👑 heroine

You understand that everyone should be treated fairly and that there is a place for everyone; but you're also strong enough to stand up for yourself and others when you see inequality in the world.

*Work it...* **You are powerful because you are:**

- Sharp
- Equitable
- Compassionate
- Supportive
- Able to make sound choices

*Own it...* **Get inspired by these kindred brands:**

Ruth Bader Ginsburg, *New York Times*

*Bring it...* **Amplify your strengths:**

Rely on your grounded morality to be your compass. Use your strength to help others and you will be rewarded in turn for those efforts.

# innovator

brilliant    X    leader

You're smart as a whip without coming across as a know-it-all, and you have the confidence to match. You're all about achieving short- and long-term goals, no matter what it takes. You always lead with the feeling that everything will be okay.

## Work it...

**You are powerful because you are:**

- Driven
- Adept
- Skillful
- Meticulous
- Confident

## Own it...

**Get inspired by these kindred brands:**

Priyanka Joshi, Bumble

## Bring it...

**Amplify your strengths:**

Things come naturally to you. Be sure to approach others with humility; this will inspire them to listen and learn from your talents. When others see your grit, you will become an inspiration to them.

*Your brand mastery*

# intellectual

💡 brilliant   X   💡 brilliant

You're flat-out brilliant. There's nothing you love more than the pursuit of knowledge—except maybe sharing what you have learned with others. You are a source of information for many.

*Work it...*

**You are powerful because you are:**

- Bookish
- Informed
- Questioning
- Energized to share information
- Polite

*Own it...*

**Get inspired by these kindred brands:**

Ada Lovelace, Hypatia of Alexandria

*Bring it...*

**Amplify your strengths:**

An enormous bank of facts doesn't always translate into wisdom. Hone in on how to apply that knowledge in the practical world. You have the ability to devise something new and original with your persistent intellect.

*Your brand mastery*

# whiz

💡 brilliant    X    ⚡ rebel

You're whip smart with an edge. You're predictably impulsive, freethinking, and highly independent. You tend to put your personal and professional values above the status quo.

*Work it...*

**You are powerful because you are:**

- One to pave your own way
- Evocative
- Fearless
- Confident
- Able to work alone or in teams

*Own it...*

**Get inspired by these kindred brands:**

*The Atlantic*, Rachel Maddow

*Bring it...*

**Amplify your strengths:**

You have the ability to see the whole picture very quickly and put your creative take on it. Your gift is your strength of conviction in your theories and assessments. You know how to communicate your notions in a framework that allows people to accept your daring ideas.

# realist

 brilliant   X   🛡 bff

You're studious and attentive, and every move you make is done with a specific goal in mind. Your recommendations are trusted because of your just-the-facts approach.

*Work it…*

**You are powerful because you are:**

- Rational
- Able to see the broad view
- Straightforward
- Autonomous
- Conventional

*Own it…*

**Get inspired by these kindred brands:**

Sandra Day O'Connor, *The Economist*

*Bring it…*

**Amplify your strengths:**

Be sure to understand your audience. Your truths can sometimes stun those who receive them. Remain neutral, but at the same time soften any harsh messages.

# Your brand mastery
# allocator

💡 brilliant　　X　　◆ gem

You may be a bit of a smarty pants, but it's all founded in love for other people (and the planet). You enjoy taking the resources you have or know of and helping others access them.

*Work it...*

**You are powerful because you are:**

- Chummy
- Caring
- Selfless
- Brainy
- Thankful

*Own it...*

**Get inspired by these kindred brands:**

PBS, World Wildlife Fund

*Bring it...*

**Amplify your strengths:**

You're a brain with tons of heart. Your messages will reach a larger audience if they are easily digestible for the masses. Learn more about data visualization and infographics to get your ideas across to more people.

*Your brand mastery*

# poet

 brilliant    X    original

You believe in the power of words and know how to use them to heal and inspire people. You continually care for others and always aim to do the right thing. There's a mythical aura about you.

*Work it...*

**You are powerful because you are:**

- Diagnostic
- Visionary
- Contemplative
- Sympathetic
- Intrepid

*Own it...*

**Get inspired by these kindred brands:**

Sylvia Plath, Gabriel García Márquez

*Bring it...*

**Amplify your strengths:**

Have confidence in the power of your creative voice. Carry a pen and pad of paper or voice recorder to catch inspiration and never miss a moment.

*Your brand mastery*

# geek

💡 brilliant    X    😎 charismatic

Your personality is smart, witty, and a little bit dorky—and you're all the more lovable because of it. People admire your attention to detail and the way you remember things that matter.

*Work it...*

**You are powerful because you are:**

- Hilarious
- Bright
- Reflective
- Alert
- Carefree

*Own it...*

**Get inspired by these kindred brands:**

Jodie Foster, Tesla

*Bring it...*

**Amplify your strengths:**

People are attracted to your casual, approachable demeanor. Others will appreciate the knowledge you deliver with wit and humor. Maximize your brand identity by mixing playful patterns and cheerful hues.

*IRL influenceHer*

# Cindy Eckert

Founder, The Pink Ceiling
@cindypinkceo

**Why we think Cindy is the perfect Brilliant:**
Cindy is the perfect example of "show, don't tell." She created and sold not one but two pharmaceutical companies for more than $1.5 billion. She's behind the innovative brand that came up with the FDA-approved "female viagra." Now, she's transitioned to an egalitarian brand that promotes and invests in female-founded entrepreneurs and helps them reach their dreams.

**What branding tips would you give to an entrepreneur?**
Be the brand. An idea that comes to life thanks to your head and heart is naturally an extension of you. Be uncompromising about that authenticity. At Day 1 and at Day 1001, no one can dictate the brand but you.

**What habits keep you on track?**
I learn something new every day and I'm open-minded that anyone can teach me. If you're not cultivating your curiosity, you're not working out the most important "muscle" you must flex as an entrepreneur—your mind.

**What's the best piece of advice you would give to an entrepreneur?**
Choose your investors wisely. Just because someone is willing to write you a check doesn't mean you want them to own part of your company. Investors who are misaligned with your vision can ruin the business. Never forget that you're choosing, too.

**Can you share some of your struggles and how you overcame them?**
Imagine me in pink, pitching the first-ever drug for women's libido to a bunch of blue and gray suits. Literally, the rooms used to erupt into middle school giggles. But underestimation is powerful fuel. I've had more than a little fun calling back some of those men after delivering 40x returns and asking them if they want in on any of my new investments. Many do, and I'd count that as meaningful change. I talk to female founders all the time about the choice to let underestimation knock you back or propel you forward. As I see it, it's one hell of an invitation to surprise people.

**Words to live by:**

# "First they ignore you, then they laugh at you, then they fight you, then you win."
# —Gandhi

**"The most alluring thing a woman can have is confidence."**

*Beyoncé*

# original

**3**

You have a kaleidoscopic approach to life and find inspiration everywhere you go. What's more, you inspire others with the things you create.

You have an extraordinary sensitivity that you channel into creative ventures. You're always striving for the new on an innate quest for novelty. You get a chill of thrill discovering new creative worlds.

You love to build and design new things, and everything you touch carries a bit of your personality and pizzazz.

**Key Attributes:**

Intuitive
Sensitive
Imaginative

Inventive
Creative
Novel

## brand mastery

**maven**
curator

**world changer**
creator

**idealist**
ponderer

**explorer**
novelist

**heroine**
celestial

**leader**
composer

**brilliant**
architect

**rebel**
firecracker

**bff**
classicist

**gem**
affectionate

**original**
virtuoso

**charismatic**
playful

# curator

 original    X    maven

You believe nothing goes without meaning, and everything—whether tangible or abstract—should be able to teach some type of lesson. You strive to educate others through the things you create.

*Work it...*

**You are powerful because you are:**

- Thoughtful
- One to think outside the box
- Sumptuous
- Creatively confident
- Inspired

*Own it...*

**Get inspired by these kindred brands:**

Diane von Furstenberg, Vera Wang

*Bring it...*

**Amplify your strengths:**

Your organization and attention to detail are impeccable. Use your collection of knowledge in your field to spark creativity in others.

# creator

original　　X　　world changer

You feel true joy when you realize you've created something completely new and innovative. You're always looking for opportunities to flex your creative muscles or make something that will change the world.

*Work it...* **You are powerful because you are:**

- Educated
- Progressive
- Eager for a challenge
- Committed
- Inventive

*Own it...* **Get inspired by these kindred brands:**

Madonna, Marlene Dietrich

*Bring it...* **Amplify your strengths:**

Don't worry about manufacturing that "wow" moment for your creation. Others will create it for you just as a result of the sheer newness of your idea.

# ponderer

 original     x     🖤 idealist

You love to explore all possibilities, personal and professional, whether in your head or in a tangible way. You live your life without regrets because it's better than wondering what could have been.

**Work it...**

**You are powerful because you are:**

- Dreamy
- Sanguine
- Inspiring
- One to work well with others
- Always excited to try something new

**Own it...**

**Get inspired by these kindred brands:**

Lady Gaga, Emily Blunt

**Bring it...**

**Amplify your strengths:**

Keep your mind and eyes open. Don't let your preconceptions blind you to new opportunities. With an open heart, you will appreciate all of life's offering.

# novelist

 original    X    explorer

You love to explore the origins of extraordinary. You express your creative side and often get lost in daydreams. You aren't afraid to take risks, and it is important to you to feel understood.

*Work it...*

**You are powerful because you are:**

- Creative
- Laissez-faire
- Known for a strong work ethic
- A great navigator
- Humble

*Own it...*

**Get inspired by these kindred brands:**

Elizabeth Gilbert, Isabel Allende

*Bring it...*

**Amplify your strengths:**

Your strong imagination will guide you to success. Explore it to the fullest in your writing and it will steer you toward new inspirations.

# celestial

 original    X    👑 heroine

People grativate toward your confidence in the universe and your creativity. You are strong-willed and aren't afraid of challenges; in fact, you think they're fun.

**Work it...**

**You are powerful because you are:**

- Individualistic
- Unique
- Strong
- Intelligent
- Proud without being cocky

**Own it...**

**Get inspired by these kindred brands:**

Nina Simone, Carine Roitfeld

**Bring it...**

**Amplify your strengths:**

Avoid questioning your ideas. Put them out there and never look back. You know the universe is guiding you.

# composer

 original    x    ▷ leader

You know what you want and you go for it. Your unique approach to things makes others pay attention. Your every detail in a project has meaning and purpose.

*Work it...*

**You are powerful because you are:**

- Creative
- Persistent
- Strong
- Tactful
- Polished

*Own it...*

**Get inspired by these kindred brands:**

Helen Mirren, Joan Didion

*Bring it...*

**Amplify your strengths:**

Be sure people get your artistically created vision. They need to understand the subtleness and meaning behind your creation.

Your brand mastery

# architect

**original**    x    **brilliant**

You are always looking at things from a unique angle. You understand that everything has to start somewhere, so you're rarely afraid to take the plunge.

*Work it...*

**You are powerful because you are:**

- Creative
- Open-minded
- A good listener
- Thoughtful
- Always striving to improve

*Own it...*

**Get inspired by these kindred brands:**

Simone de Beauvoir, Zaha Hadid

*Bring it...*

**Amplify your strengths:**

Balance your creative and pragmatic selves and learn when to rely on one or the other for specific tasks. Lean on the pragmatic to get your idea off the ground, then rely on the creative.

*Your brand mastery*

# firecracker

 original    X    ⚡ rebel

You know that you have to think outside the box to get the results you want, and you're not afraid to be unconventional. You value your vibrancy and confidence under the spotlight.

*Work it...*

**You are powerful because you are:**

- Adventurous
- Authentic
- Tactful
- Unstructured
- Nonchalant

*Own it...*

**Get inspired by these kindred brands:**

Annie Leibovitz, Katy Perry

*Bring it...*

**Amplify your strengths:**

Just let it go! Your strength comes from your originality and ability to bend and reshape rules of thought. Find your inspiration in the weird.

# classicist

 original   x   🛡 bff

The things you create are timeless. You'd rather provide a product or service that will last through the ages over one that is trendy or daring.

*Work it...*

**You are powerful because you are:**

- Straightforward
- Non-wasteful
- Someone who prefers simplicity
- One who creates things that speak universally
- Enduring

*Own it...*

**Get inspired by these kindred brands:**

Aerin Lauder, Jenna Lyons

*Bring it...*

**Amplify your strengths:**

The goal is to incorporate characteristics that are ingrained in the public consciousness into your ideas or products. Long-term success also relies on the quality of what you produce.

# affectionate

 original  X  gem

You're caring and unique in that you help people and solve problems in a snap. You put your heart and soul into everything you do, and it shows.

*Work it...*

**You are powerful because you are:**

- Caring
- Helpful
- Creative
- Hopeful
- One who has faith in others

*Own it...*

**Get inspired by these kindred brands:**

Kate Hudson, Etsy

*Bring it...*

**Amplify your strengths:**

Creating a safe space for others to find new ways to explore their own path and solutions will allow you to reach more people. Your ability to foster a supportive environment will inspire them to become more self-sufficient.

# virtuoso

 original     x     original

Your brand is 100 percent Original. There's nothing you love more than making things that speak to people and express who you truly are. Others love your creativity, honesty, and vision.

**Work it...**

**You are powerful because you are:**

- Prolific
- Captivating
- Likely to try new things
- Able to convey ideas through art
- Surprising

**Own it...**

**Get inspired by these kindred brands:**

Ella Fitzgerald, Etta James

**Bring it...**

**Amplify your strengths:**

Your gift is that you can create without even trying. The trick is to be able to capture that inspiration and systematically store it for future use.

*Your brand mastery*

# playful

🔘 original    X    😄 charismatic

Who said you have to be serious to have people take you seriously? Your rosy demeanor draws people to you and they take notice of your creativity and attention to detail. You approach everything with great optimism. You're peachy keen.

*Work it...*

**You are powerful because you are:**

- Sweet
- Playful
- Imaginative
- Dazzling
- Vibrant

*Own it...*

**Get inspired by these kindred brands:**

Drybar, Benefit Cosmetics

*Bring it...*

**Amplify your strengths:**

Your brand recognition will be remembered in the fun ways you engage with your customer. Social media, giveaways, and contests will help others participate no matter how busy they are.

# Rozaliya
# Heinen

Founder, Rozaliya Jewelry
@rozaliyaheinen

**Why we think Rozaliya is the perfect Original:**
For over a decade, Rozaliya has been on a journey of self-discovery and helping others seek answers to what they are short of in order to find their true self. She inspires, leads, and educates others selflessly. She is the Celestial who is in tune with the universe to create healing for others.

**What branding tips would you give to a female founder?**
The first branding tip is to discover what her specialty is. What is her true self and is she different than others? She really needs to reveal why she chose her business. What inspired her to do it? Next, focus on the creativity to achieve her potential and create a brand where people really understand her and take notice.

**What habits keep you on track?**
The first habit word is extremely important. Discipline. We need to be focused and create a life that's healthy. Really try and make the environment around you soft and filled with love. You need to be surrounded by people who support you while at the same time keeping your mind calm and thinking positively. Weekly goals are a must. Not only do you make them, but you have to stick to them with a concrete plan on how to achieve them. At the same time, the most important thing is to think of the big picture of how you can help people and not focus only on the money.

**What's the best piece of advice you would give to an entrepreneur?**
Practice meditation to focus your mind to have strong concentration. It will help define your role and create a path to proceed. In order to be an entrepreneur, you have to do three important things. First, focus on your body. Second, master your mind. Third, connect with your inner self. You will be able to help all of humanity by your activities. It's time now for all entrepreneurs to get together to help the world. Point the world to wisdom and love, and everything else will follow.

**Can you share some tips on struggles and how to overcome them?**
Struggles normally come from the wrong perspective. In business, we all have moments when we are down, when we are up, and some when we really have to overcome. The first thing we have to do is never give up. Be brave. Always know that if there is no struggle, there will never be achievements. The second extremely important point to remember is to really embody yourself and know who you are. Life is not such a serious place. Accept what has happened and it will allow for growth. If we have a strong concentration and focus and really understand who we are, every one of those obstacles can be overcome.

# "Listening to an underserved population is how you begin to understand them and serve them better."

Constance Wu

MAJOR ARCHETYPE

# idealist

4

You seek to find only the best in people. You're great at identifying just what people need and giving it to them with impeccable timing. Everything you do is performed with taste and care.

People value your ability to relate emotionally not as an inconvenience, but as a virtue.

You're a playful dreamer. Your curiosity and wonder inspire others and awaken their sense of possibility and joy.

**Key Attributes:**

Kindhearted
Optimistic
Dreamy

Free-Spirited
Spontaneous

## brand mastery

**maven**
utopian

**world changer**
optimist

**idealist**
lover

**explorer**
seeker

**heroine**
gladiator

**leader**
Samaritan

**brilliant**
fox

**rebel**
phoenix

**bff**
starry-eyed

**gem**
passionate

**original**
muse

**charismatic**
whimsical

*Your brand mastery*

# utopian

♡ idealist     x     ✽ maven

In your head is a picture of your ideal world, but you know you have to take steps to get to it. As a result, you are committed to helping others learn how they can improve the world around them, for the good of all.

*Work it...*

**You are powerful because you are:**

- Devoted to instructing others
- Patient
- Someone who has others' best interests in mind
- Optimistic
- Kind

*Own it...*

**Get inspired by these kindred brands:**

Melinda Gates, Hoda Kotb

*Bring it...*

**Amplify your strengths:**

Before asking others to join your journey to a perfect world, detail the specific steps to get there. Once you have that, you will be able to get others to see your vision and how to get there. Don't forget to capture the moment.

*Your brand mastery*

# optimist

💜 idealist     x     🌐 world changer

Your outlook on life and the future may be a bit dreamy, but you've proven yourself capable of turning even your wildest fantasies into reality. Your ideas always have a touch of optimism, which inspires others to follow your confidence.

*Work it...*

**You are powerful because you are:**

- Positive
- Imaginative
- Productive
- Sensitive
- Artistic

*Own it...*

**Get inspired by these kindred brands:**

Pixar, Nora Ephron

*Bring it...*

**Amplify your strengths:**

There is real power in positive thinking. Ask a trusted guide to give you a balanced perspective to keep your ideas in check.

# lover

♡ idealist     x     ♡ idealist

Your brand is 100 percent Idealist. You're dreamy, sensitive, and sweet all at once—but don't let people mistake that for softness. While you may have an affinity for sun-soaked afternoons, you're determined to achieve your aspirations, and you won't stop at anything until you have.

*Work it...*

**You are powerful because you are:**

- Considerate
- Thoughtful
- Delicate
- Kindhearted
- Gentle

*Own it...*

**Get inspired by these kindred brands:**

Petra Nemcova, Marie Antoinette

*Bring it...*

**Amplify your strengths:**

Your true power is spreading light and love throughout the world. Don't be discouraged by cynicism. Stay true to who you are and all will fall into place.

*Your brand mastery*

# seeker

♡ idealist     x     ◉ explorer

You approach your globe-trotting life with a determined positivity. What you know of the world, you love, and you love to discover things you don't already know. The fun is in the quest to find answers to what you don't know.

*Work it...*

**You are powerful because you are:**

- Hopeful
- Curious
- Sincere
- Forthright
- Lively

*Own it...*

**Get inspired by these kindred brands:**

Roxy, Nellie Bly

*Bring it...*

**Amplify your strengths:**

You inspire others through your curiosity and ability to share your unique experiences. People love to hear about your adventures. Learn the art of storytelling.

# gladiator

idealist    x    heroine

You may be known as a lover, but you'll fight for what you love. You aren't easily discouraged; instead, you keep going until you get what you want. Your drive is fueled by your beliefs.

*Work it...*

**You are powerful because you are:**

- Determined
- Passionate
- Daring
- Able to inspire others with your actions
- Strong

*Own it...*

**Get inspired by these kindred brands:**

Gal Gadot, the Olympic Games

*Bring it...*

**Amplify your strengths:**

Don't let your drive cloud your sound judgment. Your determination is magnetic and others will easily follow. But don't forget there is responsibility that comes with leadership.

# Samaritan

idealist    x    leader

Forever graceful and dignified, you always try to bring out the best in everyone. No detail remains unnoticed, and each task is done with perfection. You bring light and goodness to the world and inspire others to do the same. You're massively influential.

*Work it...*

**You are powerful because you are:**

- Quality-driven
- Positive
- Amicable
- Willing to go above and beyond for others
- Assured

*Own it...*

**Get inspired by these kindred brands:**

Padmé Amidala, Scarlett Johansson

*Bring it...*

**Amplify your strengths:**

Your magnetism lies in your timeless look, which is always perfect. To get more followers, get down off your pedestal and show your human side.

*Your brand mastery*

# fox

 idealist      x      💡 brilliant

You're perceptive and imaginative, yet sharp as a tack. It's about more than just being beauty and brains; it's also about being passionate and giving back. You're a treasure trove of wisdom.

*Work it...*

**You are powerful because you are:**

- Sensitive to others' emotional needs
- Someone who enjoys studying and learning new things
- Recognized as an expert on a particular topic
- Witty
- Hopeful and optimistic about the future

*Own it...*

**Get inspired by these kindred brands:**

Edith Wharton, Girls Who Code

*Bring it...*

**Amplify your strengths:**

Sometimes it's better to show, not tell. Throw in some data and facts to prove your case.

*Your brand mastery*

# phoenix

♡ idealist    x    ⚡ rebel

You're a lover with a catch—an unbeatable desire to conquer the status quo and create something of your own. Your passion makes you noticeably better at what you do.

*Work it...*

**You are powerful because you are:**

- Daring
- Mysterious
- Independent
- Cheeky
- Alluring

*Own it...*

**Get inspired by these kindred brands:**

Yoko Ono, Lady Godiva

*Bring it...*

**Amplify your strengths:**

Keep your cards close to your chest with a wink and a smile. The mystery surrounding your brand will keep the allure alive. Show your hand and the wonder is gone.

*Your brand mastery*

# starry-eyed

♡ idealist   x   🛡 bff

You view the world through rose-tinted glasses. You are always optimistic and hopeful, and people are drawn to your positivity. They want to live in your picture of the ideal world.

*Work it...*

**You are powerful because you are:**

- Energetically happy
- One who stops to smell the roses
- Free
- Empathetic with others
- Timeless

*Own it...*

**Get inspired by these kindred brands:**

Ariana Grande, Nora Roberts

*Bring it...*

**Amplify your strengths:**

A consistent, positive message will foster trust in your brand. An amiable disposition is what others seek most from you.

*Your brand mastery*

# passionate

♡ idealist    x    ◈ gem

You're the epitome of love and support. Rather than viewing emotional sensitivity as a weakness, you see it as a strength. People love your passion and consideration for others.

*Work it...*

**You are powerful because you are:**

- Warmhearted
- Kind
- Someone who takes care of others
- Communicative
- Emotionally intelligent

*Own it...*

**Get inspired by these kindred brands:**

Audrey Hepburn, Sprinkles Cupcakes

*Bring it...*

**Amplify your strengths:**

Others will connect with your strength and conviction in your message. Make sure your message is consistent and the driving force in your communications.

# muse

 idealist     x     🌀 original

You ooze style and substance. Your polished ease, thoughts, and ideas inspire others to dream up creative ideas of their own.

*Work it...*

**You are powerful because you are:**

- Highly creative
- Mindful
- Inspired
- Emotionally mature
- Considerate

*Own it...*

**Get inspired by these kindred brands:**

Amanda Seyfried, Miranda Kerr

*Bring it...*

**Amplify your strengths:**

Your power is that you are highly influential to how others feel and think. This is where your considerate nature comes into play, as it will keep you from steering people in the wrong direction.

*Your brand mastery*

# whimsical

🩶 idealist      x      😆 charismatic

---

You have a kind, lighthearted spirit that's easy to love. There is an air of ease and comfort around you. Your playful nature inspires and attracts others.

*Work it...*

**You are powerful because you are:**

- Hopeful
- Positive
- Fun-loving
- Quick to make other people smile and laugh
- Uplifting

*Own it...*

**Get inspired by these kindred brands:**

Blue Star Donuts, tokidoki

*Bring it...*

**Amplify your strengths:**

Zig when others zag to keep people entertained and engaged. The allure comes from your unpredictability and playful wit.

# Toni Ko

Founder, NYX Cosmetics
@tonikokoko

**Why we think Toni is the perfect Idealist:**
When Toni started NYX Cosmetics, the timing couldn't have been more perfect. NYX Cosmetics bridged the gap between low-end cosmetics and lofty-priced ones. She was able to build and sell the company for nearly half a billion dollars. Today, she's doing it again with Perverse Sunglasses. Her Gladiator drive to create two successful companies is a true inspiration.

**What habits keep you on track?**
In order to stay on track, I have to make a to-do list. I continuously make them, and they're always handwritten on a piece of paper. The key is to not make a list longer than twelve items. I cross items off the list as I complete each task. When the twelve items are completed, I make a fresh list and begin working on those tasks. A good tip is to complete the tasks in order of easy to difficult. Get the quick and easy ones out of the way first, and then move on to the next, and the next, etcetera.

**What branding tips would you give a female founder?**
Make sure your brand is in line with your own personal style. Your brand should really be something you can be proud of and something that you love. It's essential for the brand owner to truly fall in love with her own brand. Love your brand like you love yourself!

**What's the best piece of advice you would give?**
Prepare, prepare, prepare! Nothing and no one can beat a person who is prepared (besides natural-born talents). Always prepare and practice before any meeting or presentation. Do your research and make sure you know your facts. Make sure you have answers to any potential questions that might come your way.

**Can you share some of your struggles and how you overcame them?**
When I was going through the sale of NYX Cosmetics, I was "deal fatigued" toward the end of the process. It's not a small feat to sell your company—it's incredibly mentally and emotionally draining. It was extremely difficult for me to say goodbye to a company and brand that was basically my entire life. I wasn't married nor had children, so NYX Cosmetics was my everything. At one point I realized I was being overly sensitive to everyone involved in the transaction, and frankly, I was being irrational.

The best thing I did was take a three-day break from it all. I checked myself into a hotel in Santa Barbara and did nothing but sleep, eat, and take long walks. I completely unplugged during this time. I turned my phone and computer off, spoke to no one, and completely cut myself off from the outside world and distractions in life. After three days, I emerged born-again. It was only after those days alone that I was able to calm myself down and see the transaction to the finish line.

**What are your favorite words you live by?**
Good is the enemy of great. Ever since I read *Good to Great* by Jim Collins, both my life and my career have become much more positive and productive. I cannot stress enough how important it is for all entrepreneurs to read this book. Don't ever settle for "good" or "good enough." Always ask yourself, "What more can I do to improve?" Do not stop and don't settle until something is not just good, but great.

"One child, one teacher, one book, one pen can change the world."

Malala Yousafzai

MAJOR ARCHETYPE

# world changer

5

You're known for thinking outside the box and boldly trailblazing. You're driven to improve a product, service, or industry. After all, why continue to do things the way they've always been done?

**Key Attributes:**

Change-Making
Passionate
Unconventional

Resilient
Forward-Thinking

*brand mastery*

---

**maven**
groundbreaker

**world changer**
equalizer

**idealist**
dreamer

**explorer**
pathfinder

**heroine**
activist

**leader**
iron lady

**brilliant**
guiding light

**rebel**
maverick

**bff**
admired

**gem**
model citizen

**original**
avant-garde

**charismatic**
visionary

*Your brand mastery*

# groundbreaker

🌐 world changer    x    ✺ maven

You believe that setting a good example is the best way to educate others. And what better way to set a good example than setting up a foundation for future success?

*Work it…*

**You are powerful because you are:**

- Faithful
- Contemporary
- Driven to create things that are cutting-edge
- Forward-thinking
- Passionate about others' success

*Own it…*

**Get inspired by these kindred brands:**

Katrina Lake, Harriet Tubman

*Bring it…*

**Amplify your strengths:**

Be sure that your innovation fully solves a problem or improves a process. Innovation for innovation's sake is wasteful. Always include a giving-back component in all that you do.

*Your brand mastery*

# equalizer

 world changer    x    🌐 world changer

Your main goal is progress. Why do things the way you've always done them when you could find cooler, faster ways that will dazzle the world? Your brand strives to break the mold and set the stage for the time to come.

*Work it...*

**You are powerful because you are:**

- A modern and progressive person
- Highly productive
- Innovative
- Great at problem-solving
- Someone who has high standards

*Own it...*

**Get inspired by these kindred brands:**

Susan B. Anthony, Alexandria Ocasio-Cortez

*Bring it...*

**Amplify your strengths:**

Experiment without the need for acceptance from anyone. It will keep your innovation pure. Create without fear and don't stop. Make sure your creation isn't just shiny, but practical.

# dreamer

 world changer    X    ♡ idealist

You're always dreaming about what you'd like to introduce to the world next. The past is of no consequence to you; that's done and done, and you like to focus on the future. Your internal blinders help you focus forward.

*Work it...*

**You are powerful because you are:**

- Ambitious
- Inventive
- Enthusiastic
- Hopeful
- Devoted

*Own it...*

**Get inspired by these kindred brands:**

Miuccia Prada, Glossier

*Bring it...*

**Amplify your strengths:**

Your inner core is guiding you to a higher goal that you know is right. Any bumps in the road should be seen as opportunities for growth.

*Your brand mastery*

# pathfinder

 world changer    x    explorer

You love to make discoveries. Everything new you find will make your creations that much more innovative. You strive to stay ahead of the game by seeking out uncharted territories.

*Work it...*

**You are powerful because you are:**

- Experimental
- Creative
- Research-oriented
- Curious
- One to try new things to see the outcome

*Own it...*

**Get inspired by these kindred brands:**

Sally Ride, Grace O'Malley

*Bring it...*

**Amplify your strengths:**

Your explorations into the new help others realize it can be done and give them the courage to try. Help others see that stepping out of their comfort zone doesn't need to be scary.

*Your brand mastery*

# activist

🌐 world changer   x   👑 heroine

You often find yourself leading the way—particularly when it comes to creating or selling brand-new ideas. Others admire your ability to think outside the box and set a good example by simply doing what you set out to do.

*Work it...*

**You are powerful because you are:**

- Brilliant
- Charming
- Innovative
- Tough
- Thoughtful

*Own it...*

**Get inspired by these kindred brands:**

Rosa Parks, the Suffragettes

*Bring it...*

**Amplify your strengths:**

Your eye-on-the-prize, laser-like focus tends to leave others behind as you race toward your goal. Reflect and share your accomplishments and milestones along the way so that others can get behind your mission.

*Your brand mastery*

# iron lady

🌐 world changer    x    ▷ leader

You come across like a firm handshake. You have incredibly high standards for yourself, your team, and your commodity. Your vision and goals are big. The things you create are designed to change the world for generations to come.

*Work it...*

**You are powerful because you are:**

- Able to predict future market needs and desires
- Innovative
- Steadfast
- Willing to think creatively
- Tenacious

*Own it...*

**Get inspired by these kindred brands:**

Margaret Thatcher, Madeleine Albright

*Bring it...*

**Amplify your strengths:**

Your determination to reach your goals is second to none. You need to practice patience when things don't go as fast as you would like them to.

*Your brand mastery*

# guiding light

🌐 world changer    x    💡 brilliant

You're always working toward some sort of goal, and you do so in a sensible, meticulous way. Rather than focusing on the past, you like to think about what you can accomplish in the future.

*Work it...*

**You are powerful because you are:**

- Hardworking
- Detail-oriented
- Conscious of all angles before acting
- Clever
- A perfectionist

*Own it...*

**Get inspired by these kindred brands:**

Kamala Harris, Sonia Sotomayor

*Bring it...*

**Amplify your strengths:**

Your ability to see potential pitfalls is uncanny. Use that skill to help yourself and others navigate around road blocks. Periodically reassess your course of action to make sure the plan you laid out is still valid.

# maverick

🌐 world changer    X    ⚡ rebel

You aren't afraid to stray from the status quo if it means creating something new and groundbreaking. You often find yourself setting the standard for others in your industry by identifying a problem and finding the solution.

*Work it...*

**You are powerful because you are:**

- A risk-taker
- Independent
- Adventurous
- Self-driven
- Explosive

*Own it...*

**Get inspired by these kindred brands:**

Serena Williams, Wilma Rudolph

*Bring it...*

**Amplify your strengths:**

Always focus on what you're doing with your business and brand, but don't lose sight of what the competition is doing. Do your own thing and you will remain ahead of them.

# admired

 world changer    x    🛡 bff

Though you're a bit of a traditionalist, you're also able to carefully predict trends and adjust your values accordingly. You like to provide what people are comfortable with while still managing to set yourself apart.

*Work it...*

**You are powerful because you are:**

- Trustworthy
- Able to predict future needs and desires
- Comforting
- Good at exercising forethought
- Consistent

*Own it...*

**Get inspired by these kindred brands:**

Gigi Hadid, Barre3

*Bring it...*

**Amplify your strengths:**

Stay ahead of the curve by not only monitoring the trends in your industry,  but looking at those in other industries that you could learn from and apply to your own. These could be seemingly unrelated industries.

# model citizen

 world changer  x  💎 gem

You believe in forward progress that benefits not only yourself, but those who are less fortunate. You're great at getting people to believe in and support your mission.

*Work it...*

**You are powerful because you are:**

- Creative
- Considerate
- Generous
- Progressive
- Loving

*Own it...*

**Get inspired by these kindred brands:**

Gloria Vanderbilt, Queen Victoria

*Bring it...*

**Amplify your strengths:**

Others will share a stronger emotional connection with you if they're able to understand the belief system behind your brand.

# avant-garde

 world changer    x    🌀 original

The things you create have an innovative touch and always center on new ideas. Your main goal is to move the needle forward through your product or service.

*Work it...*

**You are powerful because you are:**

- Inventive
- Dynamic
- Pondering
- Resolute
- Visionary

*Own it...*

**Get inspired by these kindred brands:**

Coco Chanel, Virginia Woolf

*Bring it...*

**Amplify your strengths:**

Your originality and visionary thinking are your superpowers. Own your creative quirkiness and don't let others' opinions sway you from that.

*Your brand mastery*

# visionary

🌐 world changer    x    😊 charismatic

You spread your innovative ideas in a way that appeals to people's positive side, whether it's kindhearted, hopeful, or downright funny. These ideas are always backed by your good intentions to help the world.

*Work it...*

**You are powerful because you are:**

- Brilliant
- Charming
- Lighthearted
- Positive
- Impressive

*Own it...*

**Get inspired by these kindred brands:**

Martha Graham, Katharine Hepburn

*Bring it...*

**Amplify your strengths:**

Folks immediately engage with your message because of the newness of it. Keep the outlook positive and energetic in all your communications.

IRLinfluenceHer

# Amy Eldon

Cofounder, Creative Visions
@turteldon

**Why we think Amy is the perfect World Changer:**
Anyone who's been around Amy is drawn to her spark and light to leave this world a better place. She is the cofounder of Creative Visions, which uses the power of media and the arts to ignite positive social change in the world. She is unique in that she encapsulates every World Changer archetype. We definitely need more Amys in the world!

**What branding tips would you give to a female founder?**
Stay true to yourself. Don't shrink. Speak up. Laugh at yourself. Support each other in the workplace, and don't let toxic people crush your spirit.

**What habits keep you on track?**
I write lists. I even put things on my list I have already accomplished to make me feel like I have accomplished more.

I always marveled at women who got up really early so they could have time to ease into the day. I tried that when I was younger and by 10:00 a.m., I was ready for a nap. Now that I am a bit older I get up really early and try to figure out my priorities for the day before the onslaught of children needing tacos (yes, my kids eat tacos for breakfast).

I try very hard not to speak unkindly about others and to rise above the negative chatter. I pick one friend who is trustworthy, and I tell them all the horrible things I am thinking so everyone else thinks I am a nice person.

**What's the best piece of advice you would give to an entrepreneur?**
Winston Churchill's advice: "Never give in. Never give in. Never, never, never, never."

And from my grandfather Russell Knapp: "It's not how smart you are, it's how hard you work and how determined you are."

And finally, be kind or it will come back to bite you. As Madeleine Albright said, "There is a special place in hell for women who don't help other women."

**Words to live by:**

# "To leave the world a bit better, whether by a healthy child, a garden patch, or a redeemed social condition; to know that even one life has breathed easier because you have lived— that is to have succeeded." —Ralph Waldo Emerson

"Never interrupt someone
doing something you said
couldn't be done."

*Amelia Earhart*

MAJOR ARCHETYPE

# explorer

## 6

You lust to discover the secrets of the stars. You have an unquenchable desire to sail to uncharted lands and soar the heights of the human spirit.

You approach life with an open heart and starry eyes, and everything you do is an adventure. People admire your upbeat, can-do attitude and conviction. Is there any challenge you won't take on?

**Key Attributes:**

Enthusiastic
Inquisitive
Highly Autonomous

Eager to Experience New Things
Individualistic

## brand mastery

**maven**
scout

**explorer**
adventurer

**brilliant**
scientist

**gem**
conscientious

**world changer**
pioneer

**heroine**
bold

**rebel**
inquisitor

**original**
shape-shifter

**idealist**
open mind

**leader**
climber

**bff**
inspector

**charismatic**
bright spot

*Your brand mastery*

# scout

 explorer   X   ⊗   maven

You love making observations through thorough research or casual notations and sharing them with the world. The more you know, the stronger your brand is, and the better the world can be.

*Work it...*

**You are powerful because you are:**

- A lover of adventure
- Passionate about educating others
- Eager to try new things
- Constantly learning
- Easily adaptable to new circumstances

*Own it...*

**Get inspired by these kindred brands:**

Lonely Planet, Girl Scouts of the USA

*Bring it...*

**Amplify your strengths:**

Your brand should project a sense of wonder and adventure. Spark and inspire others to go out and explore the new.

*Your brand mastery*

# pioneer

explorer    X    🌐  world changer

When you make a discovery, you also make a connection: What reality would this revelation bring? How can you use your discovery to increase productivity or make the world a better place?

*Work it...* **You are powerful because you are:**

- Determined
- Resourceful
- Productive
- Forward-looking
- A lover of expanding understanding

*Own it...* **Get inspired by these kindred brands:**

Jessica Watson, Wang Zhenyi

*Bring it...* **Amplify your strengths:**

Always reevaluate and assess your project, mission, or business to see where you can do better. There should be some progress through evolution.

# open mind

 explorer    X    ♡    idealist

You thrive on new discoveries, whether they're about your industry or just the world around you. Others admire your passion for learning and love for life.

*Work it...*

**You are powerful because you are:**

- Inquisitive
- Upbeat
- Comfortable challenging your own beliefs
- A vivid communicator
- Trusting

*Own it...*

**Get inspired by these kindred brands:**

Danielle Steel, Audre Lorde

*Bring it...*

**Amplify your strengths:**

People admire that you don't let your ego get in the way of innovation. Show them that it's okay to try and fail because of the lessons learned from that experience. They will trust your brand more.

# adventurer

 explorer    X    explorer

Your brand is 100 percent Explorer at heart. You adore finding and learning about new things, then sharing them with the world. Nothing excites you more than seeking out the new and unknown.

*Work it...*

**You are powerful because you are:**

- Curious
- Active
- Someone who never settles for anything less
- Hopeful
- Independent

*Own it...*

**Get inspired by these kindred brands:**

REI, Laura Dekker

*Bring it...*

**Amplify your strengths:**

Your bravery to explore the unknown is the quality that others seek most from you. Most are afraid to try new things. Not you! Share your conquests to inspire others to step out of their comfort zones.

*Your brand mastery*

# bold

 explorer  X  👑 heroine

Your sense of authority makes you the perfect person to lead others. They respect your experience and seek your advice, constructive criticism, and words of encouragement.

*Work it...* 

**You are powerful because you are:**

- Accomplished
- Great at taking charge
- One who always, know the right thing to say
- Supportive of others without coddling them
- Perceptive

*Own it...*

**Get inspired by these kindred brands:**

Robin Wright, Meryl Streep

*Bring it...*

**Amplify your strengths:**

Always keep in mind that there is a person on the other side of your words. A positive light that's encouraging helps drive your message home. Your words are powerful.

*Your brand mastery*

# climber

 explorer  X  ⌐ leader

You're an adventure seeker with a specific purpose in mind. Making discoveries is the name of your game, and you're notably good at it. You don't waste time wandering around; instead, you identify what you want and go find it.

*Work it...*

**You are powerful because you are:**

- Questioning
- Analytical
- Optimistic
- Upbeat
- Meticulous

*Own it...*

**Get inspired by these kindred brands:**

The North Face, *Condé Nast Traveler*

*Bring it...*

**Amplify your strengths:**

Share your goals with others so they can hold you accountable and keep you on track.

# scientist

 explorer  X  brilliant

You seek to answer your questions and theories using a fact-based approach. You are constantly asking questions and will not stop until each one is answered through your research.

*Work it...* **You are powerful because you are:**

- Diagnostic
- Pragmatic
- Learned
- Research driven
- Factual

*Own it...* **Get inspired by these kindred brands:**

Jane Cooke Wright, RAND Corporation

*Bring it...* **Amplify your strengths:**

In your search for answers, you can get lost in the minutiae that's specific only to you and your questions. Find ways to expand your discoveries for a broader audience.

*Your brand mastery*

# inquisitor

🧭 explorer   X   ⚡ rebel

---

You're guided by your internal compass to seek answers even if it's on the road less traveled. You boldly embrace your uniqueness and don't mind standing out.

*Work it...*

**You are powerful because you are:**

- Resolute in your ideas and goals
- Daring
- Bright
- Full of questions
- Individualist

*Own it...*

**Get inspired by these kindred brands:**

Jennifer Lawrence, Judi Dench

*Bring it...*

**Amplify your strengths:**

You're usually the one challenging and asking the questions others don't. Remember when your teacher said, "If you have a question, there's a good chance others have that same question"? Be the voice for the masses.

# inspector

 explorer    X    🛡 bff

You love to dive deep into the unknown, and you often go with your gut when it comes to making decisions. You never just take something at face value, and you're always seeking the truth.

*Work it...* **You are powerful because you are:**

- Thorough
- Creative
- Trustworthy
- Known for a robust work ethic
- Handy

*Own it...* **Get inspired by these kindred brands:**

Michelin Guide, Fodor's

*Bring it...* **Amplify your strengths:**

People want answers from you because they know you have studied the issues at hand from all angles. You are their go-to source for information.

# conscientious

explorer   X   gem

You don't mind going out of your way to teach others how to take care of other people; in fact, you enjoy it. People admire your passion and selfless attitude.

## Work it...

**You are powerful because you are:**

- Brave
- Generous
- A humanitarian
- Outgoing
- Comfortable sticking up for yourself and others

## Own it...

**Get inspired by these kindred brands:**

Jane Goodall, the Sierra Club

## Bring it...

**Amplify your strengths:**

Taking action with purpose and a cause is what others admire about you. A measured grassroots approach will help solidify your base of followers.

*Your brand mastery*

# shape-shifter

 explorer  X  🔮 original

You love to seek out fresh possibilities with the things you create. Others recognize you as a fearless artist who values new and different ideas.

*Work it...*

**You are powerful because you are:**

- An incredible storyteller
- One who seeks variety
- Unconventional
- Hardworking
- Self-motivated

*Own it...*

**Get inspired by these kindred brands:**

J. K. Rowling, Sia

*Bring it...*

**Amplify your strengths:**

Your visionary ability to see what most can't attracts people's attention. Your inner circle of advisers will make sure your message is on point, focused, and down to earth.

*Your brand mastery*

# bright spot

🪙 explorer   X   😄 charismatic

---

Due to your overall confidence, you don't mind being in the spotlight and putting what you've got out there. You use your sense of humor to attract others who believe in your mission and inspire them to discover new ideas.

*Work it...*

**You are powerful because you are:**

- Bold
- Funny
- Bright
- Positive
- Entertaining

*Own it...*

**Get inspired by these kindred brands:**

BuzzFeed, Issa Rae

*Bring it...*

**Amplify your strengths:**

Keeping it fun and funny keeps people coming back for more. Your humor is all the "shiny keys" you need to get someone's focus.

# Lizanne Falsetto

Founder, thinkThin
@lizannefalsetto

**Why we think Lizanne is the perfect Explorer:**
Back in the 1990s, Lizanne became a pioneer in the food industry by filling a gap in the market. Her thinkThin bars were one of the first protein-rich, healthy, on-the-go meal options available to consumers. She was also a leader in creating awareness and starting the conversation for the gluten-free market.

**What branding tips would you give to an entrepreneur?**
1. Understand your competition: Do your due diligence to really understand your category and competition when developing your retail strategy.

2. Be focused: Stay committed to your vision and brand integrity.

3. Be consistent, be authentic, have heart: It is difficult to develop a brand with no money, so I realized early on that I needed to be consistent in my messaging, but flexible enough so that if it failed, we could quickly shift directions if the category moved left and I was moving right. Be authentic to your brand and why you developed it. Messaging that is true to the heart and consistent will help build awareness and trust with consumers.

4. This is a big one for me. Trust your intuition—almost above all else: In 2004, I had spent a lot of time and money developing thinkThin's minimalist, clean, "zen" cream packaging. My executives, distributors, agencies and the data pushed me to revamp the wrappers to something more "loud" and to use all the space available.

**What habits keep you on track?**
Years ago, I developed habits designed to motivate me day after day. I made daily and long term "task lists" that provided focus and a powerful sense of satisfaction to cross them off. Before bed, I would review the lists and communicate them to the executive team to be ready for the day ahead.

Self-care, exercise, meditation, and eating well were other key daily practices I strongly believe contributed to my success.

**What's the best piece of advice you would give to an entrepreneur?**
To entrepreneurs, I say: Believe in yourself. Never give up. Surround yourself with the best, and if you don't know something, utilize advisers and consultants to guide you.

**Words to live by:**

# Everything happens for a reason. Everything leads to something better.

**"[Wonder Woman] is all about love and compassion, truth and justice and equality, and she's a whole lot of woman."**

*Gal Gadot*

# heroine

**7**

You're a titan of tenacity. You're alluring and bold and carry the type of confidence others wish they had. You have no problem taking charge in sticky situations; in fact, people value your uncompromising leadership skills and frequently look to you for guidance.

You fight for your cause. You speak your mind. You're unafraid if you provoke. With each step you make and every rung you climb, you inspire and lift as you rise.

**Key Attributes:**

Driven                    Dynamic
Tenacious              Resilient
Unstoppable

## brand mastery

**maven**
editor

**world changer**
crusader

**idealist**
protagonist

**explorer**
trailblazer

**heroine**
Amazonian

**leader**
warrior of light

**brilliant**
ambassador

**rebel**
tour de force

**bff**
ceo

**gem**
heart

**original**
director

**charismatic**
star

*Your brand mastery*

# editor

♛ heroine     X     ✿ maven

People recognize you as someone experienced with great leadership abilities, and they seek out your wisdom whenever possible. You pride yourself on what you have to offer in terms of knowledge and empowerment.

*Work it...*

**You are powerful because you are:**

- Encouraging
- Seasoned
- Enthusiastic
- Skilled in educating others in a motivating way
- Practical

*Own it...*

**Get inspired by these kindred brands:**

Arianna Huffington, Katharine Graham

*Bring it...*

**Amplify your strengths:**

Your unique ability to catch things other people miss as well as introduce other novel ideas guides your tribe.

# crusader

 heroine     X     🌐 world changer

You're always thinking and powering ahead. People generally look up to you for inspiration, motivation, and advice for success. They know you've got your eye not only on the ball, but where it's headed, too.

*Work it...*

**You are powerful because you are:**

- Rarely satisfied
- Highly productive
- Intelligent
- Innovative
- Known to have great leadership skills

*Own it...*

**Get inspired by these kindred brands:**

Betty Friedan, Princess Diana

*Bring it...*

**Amplify your strengths:**

Your strength and leadership drive people to get behind your message. They're inspired by your confidence and will follow where you take them.

# protagonist

 heroine    x    🩶 idealist

You're known for your leadership and achievements, but it doesn't mean you don't have a soft and sensitive side. In fact, your emotional intelligence and dreams for the future are how you've surged ahead of the rest.

*Work it...*

**You are powerful because you are:**

- Spirited
- Emotionally adept
- Hospitable
- Powerful
- Passionate

*Own it...*

**Get inspired by these kindred brands:**

Anne Frank, Julia Roberts

*Bring it...*

**Amplify your strengths:**

Your strong attachment between your brain and your heart allows you to see the best in everyone. This trait will encourage your followers to never settle for less.

*Your brand mastery*

# trailblazer

 heroine    x    explorer

You love adventure, and you always know which path is best to take. People come to you for guidance, and you provide a comforting and reliable direction.

*Work it...*

**You are powerful because you are:**

- Intelligent
- A leader
- Trustworthy
- A risk-taker
- Insightful

*Own it...*

**Get inspired by these kindred brands:**

Iman, Sacagawea

*Bring it...*

**Amplify your strengths:**

Your power lies in the fact that you can lead others to new revelations. Find ways to seek out these discoveries, as you will be relied upon to always make new ones.

*Your brand mastery*

# Amazonian

♛ heroine    X    ♛ heroine

You're known for getting things done and looking good while doing it. People like to put you in charge—and that's exactly where you like to be.

*Work it...* **You are powerful because you are:**

- Awe-inspiring
- Incredible
- Spectacular
- Powerful
- Unstoppable

*Own it...* **Get inspired by these kindred brands:**

Wonder Woman, Elle Macpherson

*Bring it...* **Amplify your strengths:**

You live life with a breathtaking level of intensity and heart. You press through even if the odds are against you. You stand up for what you believe in no matter what other people think.

# warrior of light

heroine X leader

You're the epitome of power. Everyone aspires to be you: productive, admirable, and great at taking charge (and taking over when needed). Your leadership abilities are highly respected because of your boundless heart and fierce protection of others.

## Work it...

**You are powerful because you are:**

- Assertive
- Clearheaded
- Convincing
- Impactful
- Relentless

## Own it...

**Get inspired by these kindred brands:**

Shuri, Captain Marvel

## Bring it...

**Amplify your strengths:**

You live up to everyone's enormous expectations. You are electrifying and willing to take risks and be a guardian of all mankind.

# ambassador

 heroine  X  💡 brilliant

You bridge the gap between leadership and know-how. You're an immense value to your industry due to your expertise and people skills.

 **You are powerful because you are:**

- Eager to both learn and share information with others
- Highly productive
- Good at and managing people
- Committed to encouraging others' growth
- A natural leader

Own it... **Get inspired by these kindred brands:**

Anne Hathaway, Natalie Portman

Bring it... **Amplify your strengths:**

You've amassed a tremendous amount of information and knowledge. The trick now is to catalog it so that people can easily learn from it.

*Your brand mastery*

# tour de force

♕ heroine    X    ⚡ rebel

---

You're often found leading people into battle—battle against the status quo, that is. You reject norms and instead favor ideas that help the world progress.

*Work it...*

**You are powerful because you are:**

- Freethinking
- Independent
- A lion, not a sheep
- Critical of older values and methods
- Creative

*Own it...*

**Get inspired by these kindred brands:**

The Wing, Fran Lebowitz

*Bring it...*

**Amplify your strengths:**

Your responsibility is to ensure that the core beliefs you share with your followers are not self-serving, but good for all.

*Your brand mastery*

# ceo

 heroine   X   🛡 bff

You're the type of leader who upholds solid, tried-and-true values for your team, no matter how big or small. You're experienced, accomplished, and trusted to do a job well.

*Work it...*

**You are powerful because you are:**

- Robust
- Confident
- All about a challenge
- Good at managing people and processes
- Traditional

*Own it...*

**Get inspired by these kindred brands:**

Tory Burch, Marissa Mayer

*Bring it...*

**Amplify your strengths:**

Your clear vision needs to be in sync with your team's in order for you all to row in the same direction. By explaining the "why" to them and allowing them to help forge the path getting there, it will become a seamless, shared goal.

*Your brand mastery*

# heart

 heroine    X    gem

You're a Heroine of the heart. People naturally follow your example, and you use your position as their frontrunner to care for and protect them. You believe that the best leaders are those who genuinely have other people's best interests in mind.

*Work it...*

**You are powerful because you are:**

- Compassionate
- One to take charge in stressful situations
- Mindful of how your actions will affect other people and the environment
- Only satisfied when you've helped someone else succeed

*Own it...*

**Get inspired by these kindred brands:**

Mary Wollstonecraft, Christy Turlington

*Bring it...*

**Amplify your strengths:**

Don't be afraid to mix it up with your audience. They will connect with you when they see that you truly want to help them.

# director

 heroine  X  original

You're normally the type to give orders, not take them, but that doesn't mean you're cold and impersonal; your artistic side allows for emotional sensitivity and careful thought.

## Work it...

**You are powerful because you are:**

- Vivid
- A natural leader
- Productive
- Creative
- One to add a fun twist to your projects

## Own it...

**Get inspired by these kindred brands:**

Jane Campion, Ava DuVernay

## Bring it...

**Amplify your strengths:**

It's too easy to get lost in the boss side of the business. Don't forget to show your creative side: your artistic choices will inspire others.

*Your brand mastery*

# star

 heroine   X   😈 charismatic

---

You charm people with your personality and natural leadership skills. Others tend to think of you as bright, encouraging, and a pleasure to support.

*Work it...*

**You are powerful because you are:**

- Magnetic
- Happy to take charge
- Humble
- Empowering
- Known for great problem-solving skills

*Own it...*

**Get inspired by these kindred brands:**

Kate Winslet, Eva Perón

*Bring it...*

**Amplify your strengths:**

Your talented nature will always shine above the rest. Be sure to be a team player and inclusive as you rise to avoid the jealousy that comes with success.

# Liz Arch

Founder, Primal Yoga
@lizarch

**Why we think Liz is the perfect Heroine:**
Liz has learned how to step beyond personal trauma and darkness to find light and hope in her daily life. Today, she empowers others to find their own light, strength, courage, health, and resiliency through yoga and self-healing. She is our Crusader and Warrior of Light. She is the epitome of strength and courage.

**What makes you excited about your work?**
I love empowering people with tools to help them step into their great strength, courage, confidence, resiliency, and healing. The most impactful thing about what I do is that I don't really do anything; my students and clients are the ones who really do the work, and I simply get to hold compassionate space to witness their transformation unfolding. It's far more powerful for me to empower people to be their own greatest teachers and healers rather than trying to be the one doing the healing.

**Can you share any struggles and how you've overcome them?**
I think the biggest obstacle I've had to overcome is simply getting out of my own way. I've been through a lot of trauma in my life, and there were so many moments when I wanted to quit or make myself as small as possible because it felt safer to be small. Fear, self-doubt, and anxiety have been my constant companions, but rather than giving in to my fears, I make a conscious choice every day to step into my courage. I remind myself that courage isn't the absence of fear, but the strength to move forward despite it.

**Who is your muse?**
I think we should all love ourselves enough to be our own muse! I've always felt so socially awkward and introverted around others, so my work has been to become truly comfortable in my own skin. When I step onto my yoga mat, all my awkwardness seems to fall away and I feel truly graceful, powerful, and present.

**What's next for you?**
I'm relaunching my website and debuting my new YouTube channel and podcast. I also released my first book in January 2019, titled *The Courage to Rise* and published by William Morrow, an imprint of HarperCollins Publishers.

**Words to live by:**

# Maybe the journey isn't so much about becoming anything. Maybe it's about unbecoming everything that isn't really you so you can be who you were meant to be in the first place.

# "Don't be afraid. Be focused. Be determined. Be hopeful. Be empowered."

*Michelle Obama*

# leader

8

Dream. Believe. Do.

Rather than relying on external factors to motivate you, you're intrinsically driven. That superpower allows you to get things done. Your natural leadership qualities allow others to easily follow you through the toughest challenges. You don't need a title to be a leader. You just are.

Lead as if the world depends on it because it does.

**Key Attributes:**

| | |
|---|---|
| Focused | Accomplished |
| Self-Inspired | Work Like a Boss |
| Disciplined | Productive |

## brand mastery

**maven**
role model

**world changer**
diplomat

**idealist**
exceptional

**explorer**
venturer

**heroine**
champion

**leader**
paragon

**brilliant**
adept

**rebel**
individualist

**bff**
pragmatist

**gem**
upholder

**original**
tastemaker

**charismatic**
empress

*Your brand mastery*

# role model

▷ leader    X    ✦   maven

People look up to you; you're either working toward setting the standard for your field or you've already done it. Others want to follow in your footsteps.

*Work it...*

**You are powerful because you are:**

- A good example
- Accomplished
- Good at reflecting on past challenges and achievements
- Eager to educate others

*Own it...*

**Get inspired by these kindred brands:**

Sheryl Sandberg, Harvard

*Bring it...*

**Amplify your strengths:**

Share all your tips and tricks that have helped you succeed, including which role models have helped shape your brand.

*Your brand mastery*

# diplomat

▷ leader    X    🌐 world changer

---

So much social change has happened because you push and persist. You inspire others because you always find the time, passion, and energy to give back. You live by a purpose-driven code and create a wealth of opportunities for social and economic empowerment.

*Work it...*

**You are powerful because you are:**

- Perceptive of people's needs
- An agent of change
- A go-getter
- Detail-oriented
- Forward-thinking

*Own it...*

**Get inspired by these kindred brands:**

Aung San Suu Kyi, Emma Watson

*Bring it...*

**Amplify your strengths:**

You're ahead of your time. Take the time to share your world-shifting insights and talents with others so they can help you fight for progress.

# exceptional

 leader    X    ♡    idealist

You're what everyone wants to be: accomplished, kind, motivated, and easy to like. You may be out there getting things done, but not without flashing a cool smile and making others feel warm and fuzzy inside.

*Work it...*

**You are powerful because you are:**

- Highly productive
- Goal-oriented
- Sensitive to others' needs and wants
- Elite
- Personable

*Own it...*

**Get inspired by these kindred brands:**

Misty Copeland, PopSugar

*Bring it...*

**Amplify your strengths:**

You're able to shine effortlessly, which is your real strength. Always keep grounded by being thankful for your gifts.

# venturer

 leader    X    ◉ explorer

You go out of your way to discover new things rather than settling for the old. You're accomplished without being flashy or over-the-top. Give yourself the freedom to pursue ideas even if they seem unorthodox. Discover your true north.

*Work it...*    **You are powerful because you are:**

- Curious
- Motivated
- Effective
- One to value new ideas
- Optimistic

*Own it...*    **Get inspired by these kindred brands:**

Virgin Limited Edition, Jenna Lyons

*Bring it...*    **Amplify your strengths:**

Your attraction lies in your openness to accept new ideas. Adding fun and adventure to the equation, you have a great balance people like.

*Your brand mastery*

# champion

leader   X   heroine

You're always fighting for progress and the greater good. You're known for your can-do attitude, which consistently pushes you toward the next win. You can accomplish more in one day than many can in a year.

*Work it...*

**You are powerful because you are:**

- One to set high but achievable standards
- Always impressing others
- Goal-oriented
- Highly motivated
- Confident

*Own it...*

**Get inspired by these kindred brands:**

Venus Williams, Gucci

*Bring it...*

**Amplify your strengths:**

Stumbles are a part of life. Accept when you make a mistake and move on quickly. You excel at being hard on yourself. Look at failures as stepping stones, a bridge to learning. Take a step back, learn, and improve.

*Your brand mastery*

# paragon

 leader    X    ▷ leader

You set a high bar. You're the epitome of productivity, and you always look calm and collected while getting stuff done. Even the highest obstacles won't get in the way of you achieving your goals.

*Work it...*

**You are powerful because you are:**

- Persistent
- Organized
- Ambitious
- Remarkable
- Responsible

*Own it...*

**Get inspired by these kindred brands:**

Susan Wojcicki, Meg Whitman

*Bring it...*

**Amplify your strengths:**

Allow for glorious stretches of uninterrupted dreaming and playing. Let the good things in life catch up with you. These moments will energize you to continue to make a world of spectacular difference.

*Your brand mastery*

# adept

⚑ leader    X    💡 brilliant

You're a sponge for information, and you like to use that data to make informed and responsible decisions that work toward your goals. As a result, people know you as someone who fearlessly accomplishes their objectives.

*Work it...*

**You are powerful because you are:**

- Persistent
- Eager to learn
- Well-rounded
- One who likes to take action
- Responsible

*Own it...*

**Get inspired by these kindred brands:**

Susan Sontag, Grace Hopper

*Bring it...*

**Amplify your strengths:**

The ease with which you move through objectives could appear to others as hoity-toity. To be relatable, show your emotional side occasionally so others don't think you're a robot.

*Your brand mastery*

# individualist

▷ leader    X    ⚡ rebel

You don't waste time relying on others for help. Instead, you forge your own path, and you almost always succeed—even if you have to jump over a few hurdles. Whatever your goal, you stand strong—it's your determination that helps you get there.

*Work it...*

**You are powerful because you are:**

- Independent
- Determined
- Accomplished
- Defiant
- Self-motivated

*Own it...*

**Get inspired by these kindred brands:**

Awkwafina, Chloe Kim

*Bring it...*

**Amplify your strengths:**

You're motivated by others telling you no or that you can't do it. Use that as fuel to crush it.

*Your brand mastery*

# pragmatist

leader    X    bff

You're a consistent, rational force, and others see you as loyal and trustworthy. Your fans feel that they can rely on you to provide a useful product that they'll always be pleased with. You're the beating heart of your organization.

## Work it...

### You are powerful because you are:

- Trustworthy
- Calm, cool, and collected
- Reliable
- Of high integrity
- Widely loved

## Own it...

### Get inspired by these kindred brands:

Katie Rodan, Elizabeth Warren

## Bring it...

### Amplify your strengths:

Your slow and steady pace has helped you succeed in all that you touch. This is reflected in the trusted quality of what you produce. Don't forget that all work and no play makes Jane a dull girl.

# upholder

 leader    X    ◆ gem

You're incredibly accomplished, and you've managed to succeed by offering people things within their comfort zone. You know just what people want and need, and you give it to them in a practical way.

*Work it...*

### You are powerful because you are:

- Dependable
- No-nonsense
- Great at identifying others' needs
- Practical
- Service-oriented

*Own it...*

### Get inspired by these kindred brands:

Real Simple, The Ritz-Carlton

*Bring it...*

### Amplify your strengths:

You know how to connect with people and give them a sense of safety and security. They never feel alone with you at the helm.

# tastemaker

 leader    X    🐍 original

You're incredibly creative; grand ideas are always swimming around in your head, and you're constantly working to turn them into something tangible. Others admire your devotion, passion, and productivity.

*Work it...*

**You are powerful because you are:**

- Goal-oriented
- One to think outside the box
- Colorful
- Self-motivated
- Self-curated

*Own it...*

**Get inspired by these kindred brands:**

*Vogue*, Stella McCartney

*Bring it...*

**Amplify your strengths:**

You're not short of ideas, which sometimes leads to delays in developing a final product as you're constantly tinkering with it. Keep a trusted adviser who's willing to keep you honest and help you progress forward.

# empress

 leader    X    😈 charismatic

You don't have to brag for people to know you're pretty awesome—they can see it in your list of achievements. You're a friendly face, and others like you because you're humble and uplifting.

*Work it...*

**You are powerful because you are:**

- Confident
- Positive
- Hardworking
- Results-driven
- Always looking ahead

*Own it...*

**Get inspired by these kindred brands:**

Catherine the Great, Angelina Jolie

*Bring it...*

**Amplify your strengths:**

Your ability to fall down and pick yourself back up again is your superpower. Your tribe loves to hear about your journey, and how you learned from your mistakes and overcame them.

*IRL influenceHer*

# Patty Jenkins

Director & Screenwriter
@PattyJenks

**Why we think Patty is the perfect Leader:**
Talk about your role model and champion for women in the film industry! Patty shattered the glass ceiling for women. By directing the massive hit *Wonder Woman*, her work became the highest-grossing film directed by a woman and one of the top five highest-grossing superhero movies of all time.

After writing and directing her acclaimed movie *Monster*, she waited fourteen years for the story that she wanted to tell. Her conviction to always stand up for her beliefs is an example for all.

**What branding tips would you give to a female founder?**
Really ask yourself what is appealing to you in every way and follow those creative impulses. For a long time anything with feminine appeal was for "ladies only," but that doesn't really make sense. We are all universal people, and following your own barometer is all we have.

**What habits keep you on track?**
Having systems in place for remaining incredibly diligent with attention to detail, work ethic, and follow-through. I've developed many over the years.

**What's the best piece of advice you would give?**
Play the long game. And always keep asking yourself what you want out of something and why. Don't get lost in the endless goals with an outcome you aren't after anymore.

**Words to live by:**

# One foot in front of the other. And keep an eye on the goal.

"Power can be taken, but not given. The process of the taking is empowerment in itself."

Gloria Steinem

MAJOR ARCHETYPE

# rebel

9

You're a master of the unexpected. You march to the beat of your own drum. You'd rather stand out than blend in, and it shows in the things you do and create. You're confident enough in your own abilities that you don't worry about what others think—you just do what you know is right.

You only live once. Be yourself.

**Key Attributes:**

Brave
Self-Assured
Rule Breaker

Forging Your Own Destiny
Badass

## brand mastery

**maven**
icon

**world changer**
revolutionary

**idealist**
wildflower

**explorer**
experimenter

**heroine**
fierce

**leader**
alliance

**brilliant**
daredevil

**rebel**
nonconformist

**bff**
resilient

**gem**
rebel with a cause

**original**
eccentric

**charismatic**
satirist

*Your brand mastery*

# icon

⚡ rebel    X    ✸ maven

You are the model that others look to for guidance. People carefully watch your every move and try to emulate them. Your confidence makes heads turn your way.

*Work it...*

**You are powerful because you are:**

- Brave
- Spirited
- Filled with razor-sharp clarity
- Determined
- One who sticks with what you believe in

*Own it...*

**Get inspired by these kindred brands:**

Alice Walker, Soujourner Truth

*Bring it...*

**Amplify your strengths:**

You're never one to hesitate about voicing your opinion. Use unconventional methods of passing on information, as this makes you all the more striking.

*Your brand mastery*

# revolutionary

⚡ rebel    X    🌐 world changer

You like to stray from the beaten path and go for something new; the "same old stuff" doesn't interest you. You're always looking for ways to improve things that already exist or create something original.

*Work it…*

**You are powerful because you are:**

- Courageous
- Inspiring
- Passionate
- Headstrong
- Spirited

*Own it…*

**Get inspired by these kindred brands:**

Coretta Scott King, Gloria Steinem

*Bring it…*

**Amplify your strengths:**

Your attraction is that you zig when others zag. Make sure there is practicality behind your innovation that's tested and works.

# wildflower

⚡ rebel    X    🖤 idealist

You're the definition of mysterious, but that makes you all the more appealing. You're highly independent and you forge your own path; this confidence keeps people coming back. You believe in magic.

*Work it...*

**You are powerful because you are:**

- One to leave things to the imagination
- An individualist
- A believer that rules were made to be broken
- Wistful
- Never hesitant to chase your dreams

*Own it...*

**Get inspired by these kindred brands:**

Patti Smith, Joan Jett

*Bring it...*

**Amplify your strengths:**

You're not afraid of launching ideas before they're perfected. You know innovation is iterative. Just make sure you communicate that with your team so they don't feel left behind. You're usually five steps ahead.

# experimenter

 rebel    X    explorer

You're always saying "Why not?"—after all, trial and error is far better than never having tried at all. Others are inspired by your bravery and gung-ho spirit. You're always seeking a once-in-a-lifetime experience.

*Work it...*

**You are powerful because you are:**

- A lover of challenge
- Inquisitive
- Eager to learn
- A risk-taker
- Hopeful

*Own it...*

**Get inspired by these kindred brands:**

Mata Hari, Janis Joplin

*Bring it...*

**Amplify your strengths:**

Imperfection can lead somewhere unexpected. Test and investigate as much as you want to. The world will be better because of it.

# fierce

 rebel  X  ♔ heroine

You're a woman of ambition on a mission. You're a fearless champion, forward-thinking, and always all in. You're inspiring because you're always working toward the common good.

*Work it…*

**You are powerful because you are:**

- Unconventional
- Epic
- Determined
- A force for good
- Provocative

*Own it…*

**Get inspired by these kindred brands:**

Daenerys Targaryen, Taraji P. Henson

*Bring it…*

**Amplify your strengths:**

You're a magnet to others because of the faith you have in yourself. Whatever situation you're in, you know it will pass. You impress others with your conviction that you'll get to the other side. When you believe in yourself, you inspire others to believe in themselves, too.

*Your brand mastery*

# alliance

⚡ rebel　　X　▷ leader

You pioneer your own path and create electrifying change in the world. You're a relentless innovator and empire builder. You blaze a trail and inspire others to not only follow but to roll up their sleeves and help as well.

*Work it...*

**You are powerful because you are:**

- Ambitious
- Revolutionary
- Fearless
- Stellar
- Effective

*Own it...*

**Get inspired by these kindred brands:**

Leia Organa, Queen Elizabeth

*Bring it...*

**Amplify your strengths:**

As a leader, encourage others to voice their own opinions. Because you know most of the answers, you tend to cut people off. Have "break storming" sessions, where you allow your team to "break" your ideas so you can see your blind spots.

Your brand mastery

# daredevil

⚡ rebel    X    💡 brilliant

You do things others may consider risky or daring, but they're always carefully calculated based on information you've gathered. You enjoy how exhilarating each win is when you've had to jump numerous hurdles to get there.

*Work it...*

**You are powerful because you are:**

- Studious
- One who plans things out before acting
- Eager to try new things
- Always trying to be the first at something
- Ambitious

*Own it...*

**Get inspired by these kindred brands:**

Angela Davis, Chimamanda Ngozi Adichie

*Bring it...*

**Amplify your strengths:**

You're a champion at coalescing statistics and data in innovative ways that keep you ahead of the curve. Your data combined with your forward-thinking nature allows you to take intelligent risks.

# nonconformist

rebel   X   rebel

You believe an obstacle is something you're meant to go over, under, or through. You walk on the wild side. You pride yourself on forging your own path and your ability to make things happen your way.

*Work it...*

**You are powerful because you are:**

- Unexpected
- An individualist
- Persevering
- Diverse
- Revolutionary

*Own it...*

**Get inspired by these kindred brands:**

Roxane Gay, Ilhan Omar

*Bring it...*

**Amplify your strengths:**

Your tribe is fixated on you because you are always questioning and going for the long shot. Your motto? If it's broken, fix it. If it's not broken, break it.

# resilient

 rebel  X  bff

You've fought hard to be where you stand now, and others admire you for it. You break through boundaries, and you (and those who support you) believe you're much cooler and stronger for taking a unique path.

*Work it...*

**You are powerful because you are:**

- Self-reliant
- Confident
- Unafraid to stand out
- Due to be a household name (if not already)
- Inspiring

*Own it...*

**Get inspired by these kindred brands:**

Women's March, Salma Hayek

*Bring it...*

**Amplify your strengths:**

Storms don't last forever. Others continue to be drawn to you because you've always shown a certain spunk and willingness to take risks. It's okay to point to these chances you took in order for them to see the road you traveled.

*Your brand mastery*

# rebel with a cause

⚡ rebel    X    💎 gem

You're compassionate and frequently choose to protect others using new or unconventional methods. You would rather do what you feel is right than stick to the status quo.

*Work it...*

**You are powerful because you are:**

- Fearless
- One who fights for what you believe in
- Committed to helping others
- Someone who would rather be a lion than a sheep
- Fiercely independent

*Own it...*

**Get inspired by these kindred brands:**

#MeToo Movement, Emma Gonzalez

*Bring it...*

**Amplify your strengths:**

You know what to do and why you do it. Connect with your tribe so they know the passion and reasons behind your ideas. Once they understand, they'll roll up their sleeves and be eager to help you.

# eccentric

 rebel X original

You're quirky and fun, and to many, you're a breath of fresh air. You create unconventional things using unorthodox methods, and you're proud of it. You relish the quiet moments to cultivate curiosity and wonder and strive to be inspired every day.

## Work it...

**You are powerful because you are:**

- Audaciously original
- Outgoing
- Creative
- Thoughtful
- Bohemian

## Own it...

**Get inspired by these kindred brands:**

Cirque du Soleil, Vivienne Westwood

## Bring it...

**Amplify your strengths:**

Old ways don't open new doors. Part of being eccentric is being able to see details that others can't. You need to be constantly stimulated with many different art mediums. Seek out art shows, live performances, music, and other creative pursuits.

*Your brand mastery*

# satirist

⚡ rebel    X    😈 charismatic

You like to push your sense of humor to the furthest reaches, but the end product is something fresh—something others eat right up. You pride yourself on your wit. Predictability is achingly boring.

*Work it...*

**You are powerful because you are:**

- Candid
- Funny
- Flamboyant
- Genuine
- Dramatic

*Own it...*

**Get inspired by these kindred brands:**

Knock Knock, ban.dō

*Bring it...*

**Amplify your strengths:**

Your modus operandi isn't for everyone, and that's okay with you. Do what you love. Don't dilute your pull by trying to be everything to everyone. Stay true to your core and you'll attract the right tribe.

*IRL influenceHer*

# Ashley Merrill

Founder and CEO, Lunya Co.
@lunya

**Why we think Ashley is the perfect Rebel:**
Ashley is the model Rebel brand who is not only an Alliance archetype, but a strong Rebel with a Cause. She is blazing a trail in the fashion industry with her tech-enhanced luxury sleepwear line, Lunya, as well as inspiring future professionals through Girls, Inc. She is shaping how future businesses will impact change for women entrepreneurs through education and investments to level the playing field.

**What habits keep you on track?**
Through this seven-year journey, I've developed a few tricks to help me manage myself and my workload. I get hundreds of emails a day and staying on top of all that can be a challenge. I actually use my inbox as a kind of to-do list and remove everything from my inbox as I complete it. This means despite getting hundreds of emails a day, I challenge myself to maintain less than twenty emails in my inbox at any given time. To do this, I'm rigorous on unsubscribes, and I use a complete-the-easiest-task-first philosophy. This helps me ensure I am timely with my responses and that I don't miss things.

Another trick I've learned to keep myself sane as a mother and seven-year entrepreneur is to work out at lunch. Working out is how I maintain my sanity and balance out all my sedentary screen time. I am proud of the fact that this personal ritual has become a healthy team-building activity as my team now joins me as well.

**What's the best piece of advice you would give?**
Trust your gut. It sounds cliché but there are so many times that I over-rationalized a hire, product, or marketing initiative only to pay the price later. Sometimes, something or someone can seem right on paper but there is a humanness to leadership that is undeniable, an unspoken feeling of getting things right, which we are aware of on some kind of subconscious level. And while we shouldn't solely rely on it for decisions, to ignore it is a mistake.

**What branding tips would you give to a female founder?**
A clear, concise brand is one that has internal clarity on who the brand serves, how and why to do so. Codifying the target customer and inventing a singular persona for them can be a useful tool; from things like sociodemographic information to broad likes and dislikes to background to lifestyle choices. This brings the person to life for the team and makes it easier to maintain consistency of message and feel. I think developing a mission statement can also be helpful—what do you do for your target customer and why does this create value? This can help the team know where their job begins and ends for the customer. Once you nail who you serve and how, you can codify the brand experience with things like a brand book, which should create a sandbox for creative experimentation that lets people play but also provides the boundaries necessary to have a consistent brand.

# "All those things that you're worried about are not important. You're going to be okay. Better than okay. You're going to be great."

*Reese Witherspoon*

# bff

You arise each morning looking forward to brightening someone's day.

You're loved by nearly everyone because you're committed to giving others what they need, when they need it. You're a trusted confidante and unwavering ally.

**Key Attributes:**

| | |
|---|---|
| Timeless | Dependable |
| Trustworthy | Supportive |
| Consistent | |

## brand mastery

**maven**
principal

**explorer**
curious

**brilliant**
level head

**gem**
mainstay

**world changer**
changemaker

**heroine**
magnificent

**rebel**
vanguard

**original**
artisan

**idealist**
anchor

**leader**
dependable

**bff**
confidante

**charismatic**
popular

Your brand mastery
# principal

bff X maven

You love sharing information and experiences with others in tried-and-true ways. People trust your judgment and often seek your wisdom when they're feeling stuck.

*Work it…*

**You are powerful because you are:**

- One who considers all sides of an issue or debate
- Level-headed
- Educated
- Clever
- Someone with a better-safe-than-sorry mind-set

*Own it…*

**Get inspired by these kindred brands:**

*How I Built This*, Joyce Chang

*Bring it…*

**Amplify your strengths:**

Your authoritative nature means you never share your experiences if there isn't some fact-based research behind it. Weave in data when telling your story.

# changemaker

🛡 bff   X   🌐 world changer

You're an innovator in the traditional sense of the word—you take ideas and data and turn them into fascinating realities. People admire your creativity and willingness to think outside the box.

*Work it...*

### You are powerful because you are:

- Unafraid to experiment
- Someone who loves to try new things
- Open-minded
- Reliable
- Trustworthy

*Own it...*

### Get inspired by these kindred brands:

Rent the Runway, Anastasia Soare

*Bring it...*

### Amplify your strengths:

What gets you jazzed is being able to share your new ideas. You'll gain others' trust in those ideas if you show your whole process and how you arrived at your conclusions.

*Your brand mastery*

# anchor

🛡 bff    X    💙 idealist

You are a comforting, familiar, and smiling face that puts others at ease. People can rely on you for positive support and security. You're very easy to trust.

*Work it...*

**You are powerful because you are:**

- Warm
- One who carries an aura of stability
- Understanding
- Compassionate
- Humble

*Own it...*

**Get inspired by these kindred brands:**

Leslie Mann, Salt & Straw

*Bring it...*

**Amplify your strengths:**

Your grounded and relatable persona causes people to place great trust in you. Never let the quality of your work, ideas, or product slip to give anyone a reason to lose that trust.

# curious

 bff    X    explorer

You're eager to learn new things and share them with your peers. You carry a cheerful yet humble attitude that easily draws people in.

*Work it...* **You are powerful because you are:**

- Adventurous
- Fact-driven
- Open-minded
- Authentic
- Resourceful

*Own it...* **Get inspired by these kindred brands:**

Giada De Laurentiis, Suzy Batiz

*Bring it...* **Amplify your strengths:**

Your openness to never make up your mind until you have done your homework is your attraction. Others admire your judgment because they know you painstakingly examine all sides of an issue.

# magnificent

🛡 bff    X    👑 heroine

You follow rules to a *t*—you're most productive that way. When it comes to leading others, you're a bit of a classicist; certain methods are tried-and-true, so it's best that you stick with them.

*Work it...*

**You are powerful because you are:**

- Cognizant of what works and what doesn't
- Trustworthy
- Timeless
- One to prefer quality over quantity
- Able to easily get on people's good side

*Own it...*

**Get inspired by these kindred brands:**

Sara Bareilles, Rag & Bone

*Bring it...*

**Amplify your strengths:**

You are the law, and people trust you for that. Your attention to quality builds lasting impressions with your followers. Be sure to be always learning and improving your processes. What might have worked time and again might need changing with new circumstances.

# dependable

 bff X leader

You're who people go to when they need inspiration or a kickstart for something new and daunting. Others admire your ability to get stuff done with little to no hesitation. You get it done right the first time.

*Work it...*

**You are powerful because you are:**

- Inspired by quality
- Self-assured
- Organized
- Honest
- Reliable

*Own it...*

**Get inspired by these kindred brands:**

Hedley & Bennett, Jessica Alba

*Bring it...*

**Amplify your strengths:**

Keeping up with the pulse and sentiment of your audience is crucial to providing the best experience and quality of what you are offering. Utilize social media, surveys, and good ol' face-to-face conversation with your customers to get feedback.

# level head

🛡 bff   X   💡 brilliant

In times of chaos, you're a stable and comforting force for good. People are drawn to your ability to look at issues from all sides and with a sensible mind-set. Laid back and calm is your modus operandi.

*Work it...*

**You are powerful because you are:**

• Calm
• Cool
• Collected
• Reliable
• Practical

*Own it...*

**Get inspired by these kindred brands:**

Kyra Sedgwick, Rachel Weisz

*Bring it...*

**Amplify your strengths:**

You are the opposite of the saying "All fluff and no stuff." You have the ability to tune in to your audience and only give them what they need, with quality in mind. Remain focused on that.

*Your brand mastery*

# vanguard

🛡 bff  X  ⚡ rebel

You are known you to be reliable, which reassures those who favor consistency over change. When you figure out what works for your brand, you stick to it. You like to forge your own path. You're loyal to your tribe but you're not afraid to speak your mind if your beliefs do not align to their values. You're down-to-earth, accessible, and will advocate for what you believe in a tactful way.

*Work it...*

**You are powerful because you are:**

- Faithful
- Strong
- Dependable
- Straightforward
- Adventurous

*Own it...*

**Get inspired by this kindred brand:**

Alicia Keys, Erin Brockovich

*Bring it...*

**Amplify your strengths:**

Don't get too comfortable. Always strive for greatness and challenge outdated methods or beliefs within your industry. Calculate risks before taking them. Is this action worth the potential losses? How big is the payoff, if it succeeds?

*Your brand mastery*

# confidante

🛡 bff    X    🛡 bff

Your brand is 100 percent BFF at heart. You value harmony and ideals and understand that your audience does as well. You give people what they're comfortable with, which makes you immensely reliable.

*Work it...*

**You are powerful because you are:**

- Comforting
- Established
- Straight shooting
- Polite
- Loyal

*Own it...*

**Get inspired by these kindred brands:**

Kristen Bell, Jennifer Garner

*Bring it...*

**Amplify your strengths:**

Your clients rely on your trusted service or product that's established and tested. To help bolster that trust, adopt a "The Customer Is Always Right" service attitude. People will be more at ease knowing that there are guarantees behind you.

*Your brand mastery*

# mainstay

🛡 bff    X    💎 gem

People are immediately put at ease by your presence. They know they can go to you when they're in a sticky situation. At best, you'll have resources to give them; at the least, you'll offer kind and comforting words of advice.

*Work it...*

**You are powerful because you are:**

- Kindhearted
- Supportive
- Honest
- Thoughtful
- Grounding

*Own it...*

**Get inspired by these kindred brands:**

Reese Witherspoon, Grace Kelly

*Bring it...*

**Amplify your strengths:**

Your audience relies on your dependability and the knowledge that you always have their back. You're their own personal cheerleader who will be there through thick and thin. Be sure to respond quickly to your followers, as they will expect their support system to always be there for them.

# artisan

🛡 bff    X    🌀 original

---

You offer services or products that are loved by all. Everything you produce has sweet details and little features that wow your customers.

*Work it...*

**You are powerful because you are:**

- Consistent
- Sumptuous
- High-quality
- Someone who appeals to people's emotions
- Colorful

*Own it...*

**Get inspired by these kindred brands:**

Anthropologie, Garance Doré

*Bring it...*

**Amplify your strengths:**

It's the little touches and twists that you add to your service or product that makes everyone notice and come back for more. Continue to keep them off-balance with fresh surprises.

# popular

bff   X   charismatic

You deliver a jolt of joy every time you walk in the room. You handle obstacles swiftly; they're water off a duck's back. You're both soothing and energetic.

*Work it...* **You are powerful because you are:**

- Trusted
- Confident
- Accomplished
- Kind
- Organized

*Own it...* **Get inspired by these kindred brands:**

Chiara Ferragni, Sara Blakely

*Bring it...* **Amplify your strengths:**

All eyes are on you. Stay focused on doing what you're doing because it's working. Don't let negativity or others' opinions distract from your mission. Positivity and light always win out.

*IRL influenceHer*

# Laurel Gallucci

Founder, Sweet Laurel Bakery
@laurelgallucci

Claire Thomas, left
Laurel Gallucci, right

### Why we think Laurel is the perfect BFF:
It's not every day two BFFs write a bestselling cookbook and open a boutique bakery that's taking Los Angeles's food industry by storm. Laurel and her friend Claire Thomas have! One bite of Laurel's organic, grain-free, dairy-free, and refined sugar–free baked goods and you'll understand the Artisan creating delicious confections at their Sweet Laurel Bakery.

### What branding tips would you give to a female founder?
Your brand's identity needs a vision, and within that, needs to be well thought out and properly manicured. My company's journey into brand-hood was story based. My cofounder and brand visionary Claire Thomas saw firsthand the rise and fall of my autoimmune disease, and witnessed the powerful difference food made in my life. After tasting my baked goods, she convinced me that the grain-free, refined sugar–free, and dairy-free baked goods, coupled with my story, made for a powerful brand. We sat down and thought out the brand aesthetic, which we both identified with so much, followed by the brand trajectory, and thereafter, Sweet Laurel was born.

### What habits keep you on track?
My family and my self-care. I really value family time. At the end of a long workday, I try my best to unplug for at least three hours during dinnertime and bedtime with my son and husband before logging back on at night. This centers me and gives me balance. Self-care is also a necessity, and for me, working in some sort of fitness twice a week and maybe a facial a few times a month keeps me feeling like an actual human and not a robot!

### What's the best piece of advice you would give to an entrepreneur?
Being an entrepreneur takes tenacity, and there will be days when you might not have the strength and energy it takes. In moments like those, it is important to speak to a friend or loved one who will encourage you and listen to you, or do a centering activity that will help you get back in the head space you need to be in.

### What struggles have you had that you've overcome?
I've had to really grow in my assertive qualities. By nature I'm a bit timid, so learning to speak up has been hard for me. The more I do it, however, the better I become at it, so more of that learning by doing theory I love so much!

### What are your favorite words you live by?
Dewey's learning by doing! It's a learning theory I came across in graduate school while earning my masters in education. Literally every day I learn something, and reflecting upon what I've learned and using that knowledge going forward truly helps in all aspects of my life.

"No election is ever just about one issue, but I care a lot about women's rights and making sure parents have what they need to raise healthy kids."

*Chrissy Teigen*

MAJOR ARCHETYPE

# gem

11

You often put others' needs before your own and consider the greater good with everything you do. You're passionately supportive.

People come to you for love and comfort, and you're happy to provide that support.

Few are as good at reading others' needs as you are. You accentuate the positive and are always trying your best to make people feel safe and honored.

**Key Attributes:**

Comforting          Giving
Protective          Nurturing
Empathetic

*brand mastery*

**maven**
counselor

**world changer**
ally

**idealist**
companion

**explorer**
cultivator

**heroine**
altruist

**leader**
first lady

**brilliant**
dean

**rebel**
authentic

**bff**
royal citizen

**gem**
humanitarian

**original**
stylist

**charismatic**
angel

# counselor

 gem X maven

You're the type people go to for guidance, and also the type people strive to be. Your main drive is your need to help, protect, and educate others so that they can succeed.

*Work it...*

**You are powerful because you are:**

- Good at providing support at the right time
- Patient
- Empowering
- Protective
- Wise

*Own it...*

**Get inspired by these kindred brands:**

Diane Sawyer, Barbara Walters

*Bring it...*

**Amplify your strengths:**

Reach out to your network, spread your passion for your mission, and get a little wacky with your solutions. You attract others by being bold (not safe) in the service of others.

Your brand mastery

# ally

💎 gem  X  🌐 world changer

You want the future to be a better place and time, and you use innovation to effect the necessary changes. You're always looking ahead for ways to help people, whether it's now or in the time to come.

*Work it...*

**You are powerful because you are:**

- Forward-thinking
- Passionate
- Attentive
- Socially aware
- Contemporary

*Own it...*

**Get inspired by these kindred brands:**

Florence Nightingale, Quan Yin

*Bring it...*

**Amplify your strengths:**

Become a connector to help you and others unify to work toward a common goal. There is true strength in numbers. You will instantly have greater impact with more people in your corner.

# companion

 gem X ♡ idealist

Your passion is passion, as well as taking care of others. You emit love and light wherever you go. People feel safe and cared for in your presence.

*Work it...*

**You are powerful because you are:**

- A gentle soul
- Emotionally driven
- Someone who puts others' needs before your own
- Considerate
- Kind

*Own it...*

**Get inspired by this kindred brand:**

Helen Keller, California Baby

*Bring it...*

**Amplify your strengths:**

Your warmth and empathy toward others is exactly why you are the support team everyone is looking for. You find tremendous value in foreseeing the needs of others even before they know themselves.

# cultivator

gem X explorer

You are always seeking the truth and feel a great sense of responsibility to continuously do the right thing. You care a great deal about others. You reach for the best within yourself and greet each moment with possibility.

*Work it...*

**You are powerful because you are:**

- Fearless
- Known for a strong work ethic
- Caring
- Trustworthy
- A fast learner

*Own it...*

**Get inspired by these kindred brands:**

Junko Tabei, Sandra Oh

*Bring it...*

**Amplify your strengths:**

You practice sensitivity and care at times when most want to take shortcuts. Continue to work hard and provide conscientious and exceptional service not only to your customers but to your team as well.

# altruist

 gem  X  👑 heroine

You are a caregiver by nature, but you stand your ground when necessary. You are incredibly generous and want what is best for both you and others. You have faith and stare down your fears, and you inspire others to do so as well.

**Work it...**

**You are powerful because you are:**

- Selfless
- Emotionally tough
- Secure
- Dependable
- A great listener

**Own it...**

**Get inspired by these kindred brands:**

Girl Effect, Kiva

**Bring it...**

**Amplify your strengths:**

You want to live wholeheartedly in a way that honors the well-being of all people. Set an example of excellence, innovation, and quality in your industry. Be vocal about your values and beliefs even if they're not popular.

*Your brand mastery*

# first lady

gem X leader

You dramatically change the vibe when you walk into a room. You go above and beyond in all that you do. You do it not only for yourself, but for those you love. You're capable of assisting others without aiming the spotlight at yourself.

*Work it...*

**You are powerful because you are:**

- Benevolent
- Highly accomplished
- Determined
- Empathetic
- Hopeful

*Own it...*

**Get inspired by these kindred brands:**

Michelle Obama, Empress Masako

*Bring it...*

**Amplify your strengths:**

Pick one central cause and stick to it. Those who care about your cause will happily support your brand. Prioritize your goals and pay attention to your personal needs, not just your professional ones.

*Your brand mastery*

# dean

💎 gem X 💡 brilliant

You're the perfect balance of heart and smarts. You use your core values and strategic-planning skills to soar. Others are drawn to your natural ability to use your intellect and research for good.

*Work it...*

**You are powerful because you are:**

- Heartfelt
- Optimistic
- Compassionate
- Exceptionally sharp
- Conscientious

*Own it...*

**Get inspired by these kindred brands:**

Margaret Hamilton, Elizabeth Blackwell

*Bring it...*

**Amplify your strengths:**

Allow your core values to be your guide in making decisions. You have the power to help many, but it doesn't mean you have to help everyone. Balance your time wisely by choosing which causes match your core values.

# authentic

 gem  X  ⚡ rebel

You have a big heart, but you know that life is the greatest teacher of all—and sometimes you have to let the ones you love learn that the hard way. You value experience and are full of wisdom. You're a paradigm shifter and a world uplifter.

### Work it...

**You are powerful because you are:**

- Incredible
- Loving
- Unstoppable
- Strong
- Relentless

### Own it...

**Get inspired by these kindred brands:**

TIME'S UP, Patrisse Cullors

### Bring it...

**Amplify your strengths:**

You're fierce and loyal—a formidable combination. You have a heart that cares and a soul that dares. Lead with your heart, teach from your mind, and the world will listen.

# royal citizen

gem X bff

You aren't trying to look like a hero, but when someone needs you, you drop everything to help. People know they can consistently count on you for care and compassion, and you're humbly happy to be of service.

**Work it...**

**You are powerful because you are:**

- Nurturing
- Modest
- Someone who puts others' needs ahead of your own
- An advocate for the less visible or less fortunate
- Discreet and unassuming

**Own it...**

**Get inspired by these kindred brands:**

Kate Middleton, Meghan Markle

**Bring it...**

**Amplify your strengths:**

Make sure you monitor your own time to balance coming to the aid of others and enjoying your own "me time." This will allow you to recharge so that you can be of better service to others.

# humanitarian

 gem X  gem

You're a natural caregiver. Your purpose is to be a guardian and protector of the world. Your ability to walk gently and courageously on this path is renowned. You give people hope with your commitment to making the world a better place. You possess passion, courage, and strength.

*Work it...*

**You are powerful because you are:**

- Altruistic
- Strong
- Compassionate
- Humble
- Kind

*Own it...*

**Get inspired by these kindred brands:**

National Organization for Women, Mother Teresa

*Bring it...*

**Amplify your strengths:**

Use your quiet strength to your advantage. You can be compassionate yet strong. Don't be afraid to provide kind discipline. The word *discipline* comes from the word *teach*.

# stylist

 gem X original

Every day is a fresh start. You love to spread creativity and love, especially if it's through something you've created yourself. Your ideal world is one in which people get along and support one another through thick and thin.

*Work it...*

**You are powerful because you are:**

- Cheerful
- Kindhearted
- Creative
- Considerate of others' goals and feelings
- Affectionate

*Own it...*

**Get inspired by these kindred brands:**

Rebecca Minkoff, Gal Meets Glam

*Bring it...*

**Amplify your strengths:**

You have an innate ability to create, love, and nurture the artist within yourself and others. You're motivated to serve and make a difference. Find a tribe that allows you to express the creative and altruistic side of yourself.

# angel

 gem X 😈 charismatic

Your sense of satisfaction is greatest when you see others smile. Your genuine self eases others. Like the sun after a rainstorm, your radiance comes out when people need it the most.

*Work it...* **You are powerful because you are:**

- One to put others before yourself
- Optimistic
- Sweet to the core
- Endlessly energetic
- Feeling

*Own it...* **Get inspired by these kindred brands:**

Lauren Conrad, Mary Pickford

*Bring it...* **Amplify your strengths:**

You radiate joy. You have a generous spirit and enjoy sharing with and lifting up those around you. You inspire others to reach their greatest potential.

# Kendra Scott

Founder, Kendra Scott, LLC.
@kendrascott

### Why we think Kendra is the perfect Gem:

Kendra's billion-dollar jewelry company was founded with family- and philanthropy-first core values that are visible in every aspect of the business. She is a selfless Gem who cares for others both inside and out. Her company donates over $5 million annually to local and national causes such as the Breast Cancer Research Foundation and Habitat for Humanity.

### What habits keep you on track?

I have to have my half-caff latte. I'm not allowed to have a fully caffeinated beverage. They say I'm already a little too excited when I wake up in the morning so if you give me a full caffeine, everyone gets a little scared. After getting the kids off to school, my assistant comes over and we have our first morning meeting every morning in my bathroom. It's a great way for me to get my day going, and it also gets us aligned on what needs to happen. I also have a daily huddle every day, and then we have weekly huddles with my exec team. We keep them short by asking, "What are your top three priorities and what are your road blocks?"

### How have you overcome any struggles in your journey?

I think with any entrepreneurial journey, know that it is going to be highs and lows. Those lows are the bridge to get you to the next most amazing place you're going. If you don't have that opportunity to learn something from that experience, you won't be able to get to the next place. It's like I always say, they're like little bridges, these mishaps, these sidesteps or little potholes we run into are the bridges to bigger, more amazing places. We have to get through it and we can't give up in those moments.

### What's the best piece of advice you would give?

Communication is key. If you wanna keep a culture, you gotta communicate. You can't just send emails and text messages. You have to talk to people. You gotta pick up the phone sometimes. You gotta walk out of your office.

### What's the best piece of advice you would give to an entrepreneur?

I think at the end of the day, as women, sometimes we feel like we have to be female. We have to be feminine. Is it okay to be strong? We are given this instinct. Women have an instinct built into them that I believe God gave us for a reason, and we need to use those instincts to our advantage. To know that you can be kind and gracious and ladylike but you can be fierce and you can be powerful. Those two things don't have to be different. That you can be the same person. You can lead a company with grace and dignity and do it with class and create a nurturing, loving environment but you can go and negotiate the hell out of a contract. You can go in there and be fierce when you need to. You can be competitive as hell. I think that's important for women. Not to be afraid to be fierce. Not to be afraid to go in and say, "I deserve this as much as everyone else in this room," and go for it and own it.

Own your future. Be strong and know you can do it. Use your instincts.

"Never follow anyone else's path, unless you're in the woods and you're lost and you see a path. Then by all means follow that path."

Ellen DeGeneres

# charismatic

**12**

Here comes the fun! You're damned funny and incredibly personable, with a bright outlook and a great sense of humor. People can rely on you to find the silver lining in any situation or make them laugh, even after the toughest days. You get great satisfaction when your wit and magic get someone to smile. You make time to play; it's the music of life.

**Key Attributes:**

| | |
|---|---|
| Clever | Lighthearted |
| Witty | Spontaneous |
| Funny | Full of Wonder |

## brand mastery

| | | |
|---|---|---|
| **maven**<br>friendly savant | **world changer**<br>good citizen | **idealist**<br>rosy |
| **explorer**<br>open heart | **heroine**<br>catalyst | **leader**<br>influencer |
| **brilliant**<br>wit | **rebel**<br>funny girl | **bff**<br>darling |
| **gem**<br>spark | **original**<br>dynamo | **charismatic**<br>entertainer |

Your brand mastery

# friendly savant

😈 charismatic X ✿ maven

You are an uplifting spirit and a guiding hand. Often serving as a mentor, your colleagues seek out your advice even in the darkest of times. You always have a wise and kind word to say and are willing to give others a gentle push in the right direction.

*Work it...*

**You are powerful because you are:**

- Engaging
- Sensible
- Encouraging
- Able to put a positive spin on almost anything
- Personable

*Own it...*

**Get inspired by these kindred brands:**

The Skimm, Katie Couric

*Bring it...*

**Amplify your strengths:**

You're a great listener and are intuitive. You can see patterns because you know how to listen deeply. When things look down, your perfectly timed wit gets people back on their feet. You're a light of wisdom even if you don't know it.

# good citizen

 charismatic    X    🌐  world changer

Your ideas are cheerful, bright, optimistic, and progressive. Others admire your ability to generate a creative spin on an old idea. You're a doer, not just a dreamer.

*Work it...*

**You are powerful because you are:**

- Forward-thinking
- Always willing to ask, "Why not?"
- Positive
- Cheerful
- Entertaining

*Own it...*

**Get inspired by these kindred brands:**

Peloton, Rosie the Riveter

*Bring it...*

**Amplify your strengths:**

Your optimism allows you to perform and deliver on any task. As with most things in life, there needs to be a balance—sometimes it's good to hear other trusted perspectives.

# rosy

 charismatic    X     idealist

You're incredibly happy-go-lucky and thrive in an environment that allows you to dream and be a positive force for good. You approach life's challenges with a sunny resilience and squeeze out every bit of lemony goodness.

## Work it...

**You are powerful because you are:**

- A dreamer
- Easygoing
- Always looking for the bright and right side
- Joyful
- A people person

## Own it...

**Get inspired by this kindred brand:**

Kate Hudson, Dorothy Dandridge

## Bring it...

**Amplify your strengths:**

Everything starts with a dream, but it doesn't end there. Strive to set your dream on fire by creating concrete goals and you'll go far. Your strength and confidence reassure others that your plan will deliver with flying colors. The positivity and light in your conviction allows others to follow without question.

# open heart

 charismatic    X    explorer

Your arms are as open as your heart. You recognize the importance of being available to everybody around you so that you can offer a supportive shoulder whenever they need it. You're always seeking to go deeper in relationships.

*Work it...*    **You are powerful because you are:**

- Unafraid of showing compassion
- One who enjoys reaching out to people
- Ready to love
- A deep listener
- Kind

*Own it...*    **Get inspired by these kindred brands:**

Brené Brown, Rachel McAdams

*Bring it...*    **Amplify your strengths:**

It's tough to stay vulnerable 24/7. Keep your center and know that every experience will get you closer to who you are. Your highest self knows. Read *The Untethered Soul* by Michael Singer.

*Your brand mastery*

# catalyst

😈 charismatic    X    ♛ heroine

You wear your heart on your sleeve, and you keep secrets from no one. You are unabashed in telling others, "What you see is what you get." You always say that honesty is the best policy, and it continues to serve you well.

*Work it...*

**You are powerful because you are:**

- Dynamic
- Expressive
- Fearless
- Supportive
- Someone who inspires people to live out loud

*Own it...*

**Get inspired by these kindred brands:**

Kate Moss, Lupita Nyong'o

*Bring it...*

**Amplify your strengths:**

Your ability to take complex issues and strip them down to their core to reveal the honest truth is a skill worth sharing. Your raw honesty is refreshing, but make sure the delivery isn't hurtful.

# influencer

 charismatic    X    ⚑ leader

You're an incredibly likable leader and are known to attract valuable connections and success. Obstacles rarely block you from achieving your goals; instead, you find silver linings and let your troubles roll right off your back. You're loyal and stand by your squad.

*Work it...*

**You are powerful because you are:**

- Optimistic
- Someone who perseveres even when faced with major hurdles
- One who gets things done
- Confident
- Diplomatic

*Own it...*

**Get inspired by these kindred brands:**

Kylie Jenner, Olivia Palermo

*Bring it...*

**Amplify your strengths:**

You didn't set out to be a leader; you were diligent and one day woke up with followers. You attract the right people because of your effervescent nature.

# *Your brand mastery*
# **wit**

😈 charismatic    X    💡 brilliant

You are quick to the draw with new ideas and a sense of what works in every situation. You gladly explore new possibilities on the rare occasion your first thought doesn't work out. You motivate others to form their own ideas.

*Work it...*

**You are powerful because you are:**

- Ingenious
- Someone who draws attention to yourself
- Witty
- Impressive
- Considerate

*Own it...*

**Get inspired by these kindred brands:**

Candice Bergen, Mindy Kaling

*Bring it...*

**Amplify your strengths:**

Keep your mind open and free so that ideas flow seamlessly through you. Brain teasers to keep the mind fresh and active will help. Never underestimate a good night's sleep, too!

## Your brand mastery
# funny girl

😈 charismatic  X  ⚡ rebel

You have a good sense of humor, but that doesn't mean you put up with things that go against your core values. Instead, you forge a path that allows you to stand up for what you believe in.

*Work it...* **You are powerful because you are:**

- Fearless
- Whimsical
- Scrappy
- Deliciously fun
- Subversive

*Own it...* **Get inspired by these kindred brands:**

Rebel Wilson, Margaret Cho

*Bring it...* **Amplify your strengths:**

Tie humor to a message or cause. Your audience will better soak in and retain your message as they laugh and enjoy themselves.

*Your brand mastery*

# darling

😈 charismatic  X  🛡 bff

You see the value of coming together and encourage others to use their strengths in ways that benefit the greater good. You are often the first to volunteer for tough tasks, and you have every bit of confidence that a solution is possible if you work as a team.

*Work it...*

**You are powerful because you are:**

- A peacemaker
- Someone who recognizes others' strengths
- One with a can-do attitude
- Present
- Upbeat

*Own it...*

**Get inspired by these kindred brands:**

Drew Barrymore, Keira Knightley

*Bring it...*

**Amplify your strengths:**

Your natural ability to bring harmony to a situation makes you the ultimate team player. It's your job to find the common thread that connects each member of your audience so that they can all unify around it.

# spark

 charismatic    X    ◆ gem

You use positivity and a healthy dose of humor to fix tricky situations—and even to improve ones that are already okay. Your optimistic nature reminds everyone to go easy on themselves.

*Work it...*

### You are powerful because you are:

- One to find a silver lining in every situation
- Lighthearted
- Playful
- Delightful
- Tasteful

*Own it...*

### Get inspired by these kindred brands:

Tina Fey, *SuperSoul Sunday*

*Bring it...*

### Amplify your strengths:

Your loving nature makes you approachable and popular among your peers. Use empathy and humor in uncomfortable situations. You're a keen observer and can discern exactly what to say and when to say it.

# dynamo

 charismatic    X     original

You are always ready with a clever joke and take every opportunity to make others laugh. You are sunshine on a rainy day, and you are passionate about everything you do. When you're not actively lighting up a room, you're coming up with ways you can in the future.

## Work it...

**You are powerful because you are:**

- Eclectic
- Creative
- Perceptive
- Effervescent
- Ardent

## Own it...

**Get inspired by these kindred brands:**

Amy Poehler, *The New Yorker* comics

## Bring it...

**Amplify your strengths:**

You like to push outside your brand's comfort zone. While your brand doesn't need to stay the same, it does need to feel consistent. Consult your brand style guide regularly to make sure your brand stays focused.

*Your brand mastery*

# entertainer

😈 charismatic X 😈 charismatic

---

You enjoy the limelight. You revel in the stage of life. Your good humor is addicting—it gets people through even the most harrowing situations. It's all about hearing the laughter from others.

*Work it...*

**You are powerful because you are:**

- Boldly entertaining
- Hysterical
- Wicked smart
- Vivacious
- Carefree

*Own it...*

**Get inspired by these kindred brands:**

Ellen DeGeneres, Ali Wong

*Bring it...*

**Amplify your strengths:**

Boldly go where others wouldn't dare. You want them to say, "Oh no she didn't!" It'll keep people on their toes. Dance like no one's watching. Pump up your brand with punchy motifs.

IRL influencer

# Tamara Loehr

Founder, Dollar Beauty Tribe
@loehrblend

**Why we think Tamara is the perfect Charismatic:**
Tamara is the lighthearted free spirit that is our Rosy, Good Citizen with a Midas touch. Musician, real estate investor, marketing guru, and now ethical wellness products investor, she has shown no limit to her dynamic talents.

**What habits keep you on track?**
In business, I follow Rockerfeller Habits. I always have a five-year BHAG (Big Hairy Audacious Goal) that I break down into three- and one-year goals. This creates a monthly scorecard for me to focus on. This provides me the discipline and focus to achieve the results. In life, try not to overcomplicate things. I am clear in what my values are, what serves me (and what doesn't), and then I "blend." I also have a monthly ritual of completing full moon intentions, which I revisit throughout the month.

**What branding tips would you give to a female founder?**
A brand is no longer a logo or a slide deck. It is something you deeply believe in and connects you with your tribe. Take the time to clearly define your "why" and get great at articulating it. Your why should reinforce your core values. If there is a conflict, it is not sustainable. Be authentic, vulnerable, and abundant. You need to become a story teller and relate. Be generous in sharing your insights, ensuring you are adding tremendous value. Keep it professional and go share it with the world.

**What are your favorite words you live by?**
Purpose. Passion and intention. Do the opposite!

**What's the best piece of advice you would give?**
First find your tribe, aka find like-minded people who share your values. My tribe are entrepreneurs. My tribe are people who challenge me. If I'm not a little fish in a big pond, I'm not happy. Then once you've grown into that space, change ponds.

Second, seek out a mentor and business coach. I always aim to have both. Lastly, one of my favorite sayings from Warren Rustand is, "You are not a success in business if you fail at home."

**What's next for you?**
I believe entrepreneurs will fix the world's problems, not governments. I believe in profit and purpose aligned to the global sustainability goals. I'm leading by example. I've started a new business called the Dollar Beauty Tribe. It's a solution for all women who have paid money and bought products they've been disappointed with. Instead, I've reversed the model. We allow you to try products (a full sized product not just a sample) before you buy them. I curate the best of the best products that relate to skincare, haircare, nutrition, and wellness, ensuring they are ALL vegan, cruelty-free, and ethical.

# archetype speak

Often in work and life you'll find you're not speaking the same language as the other archetypes—either they tune out or misunderstand or it's just not getting through. Here's our guide to help understand how your fellow brand bosses actually communicate.

 **Mavens** like to know what you're looking for so that they can provide you with something useful. Be prepared to ask questions related to their expertise. (And say thank you. Later, express how you've used their advice—you'll make their day.)

 **Brilliants** typically prefer not to use a lot of fluffy adjectives and feeling words in communication. Cut to the chase. Well-organized lists and bullet points with supporting data is what they crave.

 **Originals** want to feel as if they've had time to really brainstorm and explore all options before making a decision. Either provide them with options or give them time (and a deadline) to come up with some of their own.

 **Idealists** are sensitive to negativity (how they would view straight-talk). Start with the positives and address areas of improvement as "opportunities for growth." Show your confidence in them.

 **World Changers** are already three steps ahead in making their ideas reality before you even hear about it. Express your concerns, but know that they've got to test it out for themselves first. They'll be full speed ahead, so check in with them for progress updates.

 **Explorers** are all about the journey and an abstract idea of the destination. Leave something to the imagination to keep them interested on the path you'd like them to follow.

*hollah!*

**Bonus: Archetype Preach!**
What do the other archetypes have to teach us?

*Get more tips on the Orange & Bergamot website.*

 **Heroines** like to make bold proclamations and be the top dog in most situations. If you can give them the space to do so in a few select areas, they'll feel and perform at their best.

 **Leaders** enjoy feeling like they're accomplishing something, anything. They despise wasting time. Make sure they get to check off tasks (even small ones) toward a larger goal. And get your tasks done, too; they'll respect you for it.

 **Rebels** love to question everything. And be prepared that they won't accept your answer at face value. Better to present them with a pain point and your thoughts and let them come to the rescue with their own solutions.

 **BFFs** are very service-oriented. They like to know that you feel you can rely on them. But they value the same from you. So do what you say you'll do, keep them posted, and be consistent and reliable.

 **Gems** want to help. They need to feel useful and appreciated. Take time to tell or show them how they've done so and thank them. Ask them how you can help, too (but know they will decline; it's the gesture that counts for them).

 **Charismatics** are the ultimate people-wooers. They live to win you over. They're not ones to dwell on negative situations, so if you're looking for someone to commiserate with you, you're looking in the wrong place. Crack a smile for them and you'll make them happy.

# Business & the Brand

How do you win in business? By making branding just as important as your product or service. Branding consistently helps you shine. Branding effectively helps you win. Check out the following tips and watch your business soar. As you get comfortable with your brand, I encourage you to come up with creative ways to market yourself and your business. Share with us what you do and how you inspire others at inspire@obtribe.com.

**Brand tip #1**

Delight and inspire with brand surprises. Example: Hide a message at the bottom of your packaging. Add an inspirational quote to your agenda or underneath your email signature.

**Brand tip #2**

Get advice from your creative friends on how you can improve your branding.

**Brand tip #3**

Timing is key, so time your social media content and newsletters to release to the right audience.

**Brand tip #4**

Own your brand colors. Splash these colors in your conference rooms and all around the office. Consistently use your branding colors everywhere.

**Brand tip #5**

Clean up your act. Check your office space, including conference rooms and bathrooms. This speaks volumes about your brand.

**Brand tip #6**

Create a pretty brand board of inspiration. Hang it in your office and show it off!

**Brand tip #7**

Take field trips to inspiring places and companies to gain motivation.

**Brand tip #8**

Talk like a human. Remove jargon and overly pretentious speech from your website, social media platforms, and brochures.

**Brand tip #9**

Learn as much as you can about branding! Attend a local brand workshop if one is available in your area or watch online videos on branding from the comforts of home.

**Brand tip #10**

Review and evaluate your inventory of branding creatives. Make sure it's cohesive and congruent to your brand philosophy. Example: Do you have a favicon (favorite icon) that matches your brand? Remember, the details count.

Thank You

for the inspiration

# grateful

To the millions of female founders born ready to change the world, thank you.

I'm so incredibly grateful to my amazing team at Orange & Bergamot, Soo Kim, Chris Figueroa, and Ryan Penarroyo, and for my mentors who have been with me from the beginning, David Whelan and RJ Jones.

This project would have not seen the light of day without my powerhouse agent, Colleen O'Shea, and the meticulous team at HarperCollins, Marta Schooler, Soyolmaa Lkhagvadorj, Lynne Yeamans, and Suzy Lam.

A big warm thank you to the twelve incredible influencers who I'm utterly inspired by: Liz Arch, Cindy Eckert, Amy Eldon, Lizanne Falsetto, Laurel Gallucci, Rozaliya Heinen, Patty Jenkins, Toni Ko, Tamara Loehr, Ashley Merrill, Lauren Messiah, and Kendra Scott.

Thanks to the countless friends, mentors, and entrepreneurs who have helped and inspired me along the way and to those from the Entrepreneurs' Organization (EO) and National Association of Women Business Owners.

I'm abundantly grateful for the people on my forum #KillingIt2.0: Sameer Bhatia, Andy Cheng, Eddie Espinosa, Cindy Flynn, Daisy Jing, Trevor Henson, Amanda Ma, Quan Gan; Mission X Forum: Steve Diels, Scott Egan, Mike Gehring, Margalit Grunberger, Jeff Koz, Neil Levitt, Ramin Noghreian, Jim Winett; Entrepreneurs' Masters Program MIT Accountability Group: 1% Ninja Forum: Steve Gatena, Ken Polanco, Bin Yu, Chad Zdenek. I'm forever indebted to you for your gestalt, advice, encouragement, and supporting me throughout my entrepreneurial journey.

To my best friend and Luxe Link business partner, Rossella Ceruti, thank you for inspiring me with your brilliance.

My parents, Ederlina and Florante Nacion, for always believing in me.

And most importantly to my dearest family, Rodney, Malia, Kailani—thank you for inspiring me to be and to do my best every day. I love you!

xoxo

Kalika

# "You've always had the power, my dear."

Glinda the Good Witch

Little Brand Book. Copyright © 2018, 2020 by Orange & Bergamot, Inc. Book cover design by Chris Figueroa. Illustrations copyright © 2018 by Soo Kim.

HarperCollins books may be purchased for educational, business, or sales promotional use. For information please email the Special Markets Department at SPsales@harpercollins.com.

Published in 2020 by
Harper Design
*An Imprint of* HarperCollins*Publishers*
195 Broadway
New York, NY 10007
Tel: (212) 207-7000
Fax: (855) 746-6023
harperdesign@harpercollins.com
www.hc.com

Distributed throughout the world by
HarperCollins*Publishers*
195 Broadway
New York, NY 10007

ISBN 978-0-06-295691-0

Printed in Malaysia
Library of Congress Control Number: 2019937750

First Printing, 2020